# IRISH GARDENS

# IRISH GARDENS

Olda FitzGerald

*Photography by* Stephen Robson    *Illustrations by* William Pounds

conran
OCTOPUS

Dedication
*This book is for Desmond*

Acknowledgements
First of all I should like to thank Helen Dillon for all her enthusiasm and
encouragement and for inspiring me to be brave enough to begin this book.
I should also like to thank Charles Nelson without whose support I could
never have finished it; for his patient and wise advice, and also for his reading
of the text. Keith Lamb and Paddy Bowe who both encouraged and instructed
me, and were generous with their time and knowledge. Jim Reynolds for
cheering me on and for persuading me that he thought I could do it, and
Finola Reid for giving me her time and attention just when she had broken
her wrist. Derek Hill who was invaluable in sharing his memories of
Glenveagh, Patrick and Anthea Forde, Thomas and Valerie Pakenham, Moira
Ryan, Lindy Dufferin, Rose Talbot, Anne Crookshank, Arthur Shackleton,
Ailbhe de Buitléar, Mary-Louise Clarke of Kilfane, George Stacpoole,
Val Dillon, Terence Reeves-Smyth, Desmond and Penny Guinness, George
Gossip, Brendan and Alison Rosse, Helen O'Neill, and many others who
all formed a solid mass of support. The Director and the Librarian of the
National Botanic Gardens, Glasnevin, who gave me every assistance in my
researches, and also the staff of the Irish Architectural Archive. My thanks
are also due to the many owners, managers, and gardeners, (too many alas
to mention here) who have all welcomed me with enormous generosity
and hospitality to their gardens and been a fund of help and information.

Above all I would like to thank the people whose lives were made that
much more difficult by my distraction – Mary Reade for protecting me at
every turn, Rachel and Bob Duff for making it possible for me to work at
Glin undisturbed, Thomas Wall for carrying on in the garden with no support,
Mary and Martin Foley and Larry Power for all their reassurance. Nancy Ellis
for her advice. Anne and Peter Hosking for their vital aid at crucial moments.
Vanda and Eduardo Pissarro for their assistance. Above all of course,
my family. My mother, Georgina Willes for putting up with me and having me
to stay for months, and my children, Catherine Durham for all her very
constructive help with Glin and her map-making, Nesta FitzGerald for her
many astute suggestions and tracking down of sources, and Honor FitzGerald
for seeing that I was fed and looked after in Dublin. The most important
person of all has been my husband Desmond who has helped me with
his knowledge of the subject throughout, and without whose endless
resourcefulness, constant encouragement, understanding, and sense
of humour I should never have survived.

Olda FitzGerald, Glin. 1999

List of Irish Gardens

# CONTENTS

# INTRODUCTION

I hope that opening this book will be like opening the lid of a box filled with such delights that no one who looks inside will be able to resist exploring the glories of these different Irish gardens. Not only are they all places of great beauty, but they also show the colourful and absorbing history of Irish plants and gardens. In each chapter I have explored a single garden, and have attempted to reveal its deeper secrets. It has been a journey through time as well as space – each garden represents at least a lifetime's work, and knowledgeable gardeners have helped me at every turn to listen to the voices of the past. It has been an exciting – sometimes painful – challenge to select only 20 out of the many gardens that are open to the public. Given the problem of choice, I have selected gardens that are not just personal favourites, but ones whose design clearly illustrates a particular period of garden history, and whose plantings demonstrate an almost obsessional love of plants and the surrounding Irish landscape.

*Previous page, main picture: The rushing water of the river Camcor in front of Birr Castle seen through cherry blossom on leafless branches in early spring.*

*Previous page, detail: The deep blue of massed banks of this hollyhock in the Walled Garden at Glin Castle in June.*

Many of the gardens featured have benefited from the extraordinary number of exotic plants that became available on the return of the great plant-hunters in the late nineteenth and early twentieth centuries, and by the theories of naturalistic gardening propounded by the irascible Irishman, William Robinson. Others have combined the formal with the informal, and yet others have concentrated on the discovery and preservation of gardens that had either been hidden for many years or were about to disappear into the jungle. Every garden featured has a story to tell and the gardeners who created or resurrected them are the heroes and heroines of these stories. All the gardeners I met or researched in the writing of this book combine an iron determination with a wild but discriminating enthusiasm.

Much has been lost in the turbulent passage of time, but, in remarkable instances of tenacity, the gardens of Killruddery, Birr Castle, Derreen,

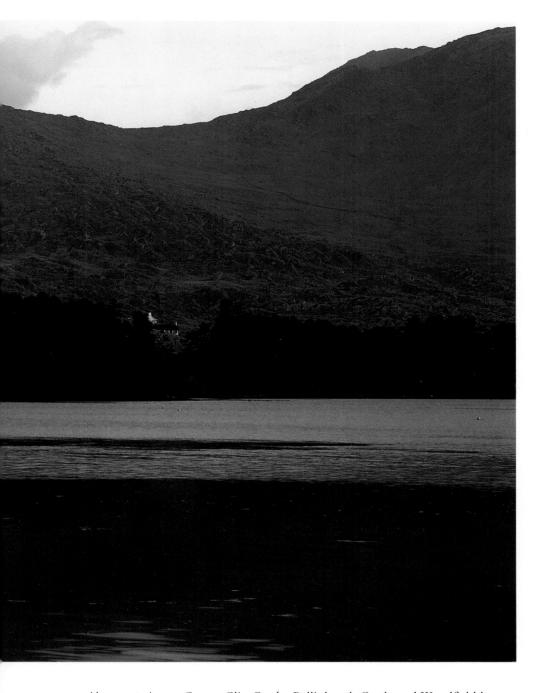

Altamont, Annes Grove, Glin Castle, Ballinlough Castle and Woodfield have been saved and, in some cases, recreated by the families who have always owned them. The National Botanic Gardens at Glasnevin and the gardens of Glenveagh Castle and Ilnacullin have been taken into the fostering care of Dúchas, the Heritage Service of the Department of Arts, Heritage, Gaeltacht and the Islands, while those at Mount Stewart and Rowallane are in the dependable hands of the National Trust. Ardcarraig, Butterstream and The Dillon Garden are gardens made by the living owners, while Mount Usher, Creagh, Ballymaloe Cookery School and Kilfane are gardens of the past, cared for by the people who have imaginatively resuscitated them.

Gardening in Ireland has a long and chequered history. In the Iron Age, the Celts made a list in severe hierarchical fashion of the trees and shrubs they considered to be the chieftains, commoners and peasants, according

to their usefulness and strength, from the great oak down to the completely disregarded wild rose. Standing in my own garden at Glin Castle, I take great comfort in the fact that, looking round, I can see each tree on the early Celtic list flourishing happily, either within the trimmer boundaries of cultivation or growing wild in hedge and woodland, and I feel a curiously visceral link with those first stubborn cultivators of this rich but sodden soil.

The Romans called Ireland *Hibernia* (Winter), but never crossed the Irish Sea to find out if this assumption was true. It is safe to assume, therefore, that gardening began to filter through from Europe with the advent of Christianity and the arrival of the Roman-educated followers of St Patrick. The Venerable Bede (673–735) wrote: 'Ireland is far more favoured than Britain by latitude and by its mild and healthy climate ... no need to store hay in summer ... snow rarely lies more than three days ... nor reptiles, no snake can exist here ... milk and honey ... no lack of vines.' The effect of the warm waters of the Gulf Stream washing the coasts of the island was clearly making itself felt then as now. The warm southwest winds maintain the mild damp climate, which means that plants and trees from all over the world do spectacularly well. The lushness and maturity of gardens created in just a few years can be astounding.

Early monastic settlements in the seventh and eighth centuries were surrounded by enclosures, within which were grown peas, beans and leeks, as well as staple agricultural crops of wheat, oats and barley. There were apple trees and beehives and 'proper, rich, edible nuts', according to Maedoc of Ferns. Maolan, an early Irish lyricist, sings of the nuts and berries and apple trees near to his hut and of the honeysuckle and strawberries. In Clonmacnoise, County Offaly, a gardener was surnamed Fionnscolaigh because of 'the abundance of white flowers in his tyme'.

The early missionary monks must have brought seeds and plants when they returned from their studies in the great schools of learning on the Continent. Woad, for example, was used to produce the blue dye for the scribes to use in their meticulously illuminated manuscripts of the Holy Scriptures. When looking at the ruins of the great monasteries and abbeys, it is easy to imagine their sheltered fruitful gardens and self-sufficient communities. Our Lady of the Fertile Rocks at Corcomroe in the Burren is a Cistercian abbey, where the beautiful limestone capitals of the columns are carved each with a different flower, in what are the earliest botanical carvings in Western Europe, dating from 1205. The Irish medieval complex would have included different enclosures for vegetables, flowers and herbs. As well as beehives, fishponds, a dovecote and an orchard of apples and pears, the abbots' and scribes' gardens would have been surrounded, if possible, by a deerpark. Hunting wild deer was a favourite sport and the medieval Irish deerpark was the precursor of the eighteenth-century Irish landscape park, such as Ballyfin, County Laois.

After the Norman Conquest, the Norman families built their tower houses and settled down, becoming, as the saying goes, 'more Irish than the Irish themselves', their military experience reflected in the efficient organization of their estates. Fishponds and warrens teemed with life, deer ran in the oak-

*Opposite: The turrets and battlements of Lismore Castle seen through the boughs of a fruitful crab-apple tree in one of the oldest gardens in the country.*

*Below: A walk of ancient yews at Lismore Castle.*

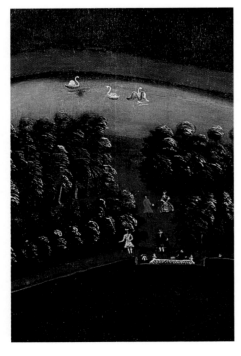

paled park and there were walled falconries. In 1238, a gardener at Old Ross in County Wexford was paid for bedding out herbs and leeks, and the impression is gained of a complex of enclosed gardens surrounding the great central court of the manor.

The first written work on gardening in the English language by 'Master Jon Gardener' was copied by a fourteenth-century scribe in County Kildare. It mentions lilies, roses, lavender, camomile and rosemary and 'all the herbs of Ireland'. Although gardening was well established by the mid-sixteenth century, it took a while for interest in native plants to spread. In the 1580s, Lord Leicester and Mr Secretary Walsingham began to grow saplings of the newly discovered rarity, the strawberry tree (*Arbutus unedo*), sent to them from Killarney. Legend has it that Sir Walter Raleigh introduced the potato into Ireland. He is also said to have brought sweetly scented wallflowers from the Azores and the tobacco plant from America, and grown them all in the walled garden at his Elizabethan house, Myrtlegrove in Youghal, County Cork, which still exists. The Great Earl of Cork, ancestor of the present owner, the Duke of Devonshire, bought Lismore Castle from Sir Walter in 1626, and created what is now one of the oldest gardens in the country.

At the end of the seventeenth century, exotic trees were already being planted in the great demesnes and the first primitive greenhouses were built. New varieties of shrubs were imported, including the variegated ones which were called gilt box and gilt holly. In 1692, Sir Arthur Rawdon of Moira in the north of Ireland filled his conservatory with 1,000 tropical plants, which he had sent his gardener to search for and bring back from Jamaica. A physic garden had been started on the campus of the University of Dublin and, by the 1720s, it contained plants from distant countries, including Africa.

The word 'demesne' is a uniquely Irish term which has survived from medieval times. It was used to describe the lands surrounding a manor that were kept by a lord for his use, so that the demesne remained a distinct entity until the early twentieth century when the Windham Land Acts finally dismantled the Irish estate system. The demesnes of Ireland occupy a central place in the evolution of the landscape, comprising areas of architectural, archaeological and botanical importance. Their distinctive layouts, which incorporate farmland, gardens, woods and buildings, still form a dominant manmade component of the landscape.

After the Restoration in 1660, the size of formal garden layouts increased to provide suitable settings for the mansions being built in Ireland at the time. Influences flooded in from the Continent through Holland and France and, in the 1690s, Renaissance ideas had caught the imagination of the great landowners. Contemporary paintings show great houses surrounded by a dense mesh of radiating and converging avenues planted out across the surrounding parkland. It was only from an elevated perspective that a proper idea could be given of the unity of the overall design, and thereby the extent of the wealth and control of the owner through his 'geometry of power'. In these pictures, it is enthralling to see the details of canals with swans and of fountains, mounts overlooking terraces and tiny figures walking in the groves.

Gardening style is also influenced by changing fashions as much as time, and when Queen Anne removed the elaborate parterres from the garden of Hampton Court in 1703, at once a similar fate befell the flowers and boxwood hedging in front of the Irish houses. Embroidered patterns of boxwood, coloured gravel and flowers were wiped away in favour of a simpler parterre of panels and slopes of mown grass outlined by gravel. Ironically, at the moment when horticulture was reaching a new height of interest, flowers were banished to walled gardens. There were flower clubs, however, whose members met in taverns once a month in Dublin, competing for prizes offered for the best auriculas and polyanthus raised from seed.

The fashion for formal gardens spread all across the country. Typically, owners would look across their boxwood knot gardens, and through the wrought iron gates in the wall and down along a distant tree-lined vista to a canal and circular pond. Everyone who was anyone had canal *à la Versailles*. The earliest and most complete surviving garden of this date is at Killruddery. In the north of Ireland, Antrim Castle, home of Lord Massareene, is nearly as old. Mrs Delany was to note faintly disparagingly in 1758: 'Lady Massareene

*Opposite top: Ballyfin, Co. Laios by Thomas Roberts, engraved by Thomas Milton in his* Views from the Different Seats...in Ireland *1783–1793.*

*Opposite bottom: Detail of the panoramic view of* Stradbally Hall, Co. Laios. *(Private Collection) c.1740.*

*Above: This plate from Thomas Wright's* Grotesque Architecture *published in 1767 was the inspiration for the rustic arch at Belvedere, Co. Westmeath.*

*Above: The sun shining on the toy fort called 'Gibralter' in the middle of the lake at Larchill, Co. Kildare.*

lives there in a very old house, the garden reckoned a fine one 40 years ago, high hedges and long narrow walks'. At Pakenham Hall, now Tullynally Castle, home of the Pakenham family, the outlines of the lost formal layout of avenues and canals can just be seen stretching away from the house and are visible in very dry summers through the grass of the front field.

Gradually, the landed estates were established and the face of the countryside was transformed by the agricultural improvements of drainage, enclosure, road-making and fertilization. Fashions changed again, and all the geometric designs were swept away, walls and hedges were broken down to let in the countryside – nature and the serpentine line were all the rage. The walled fruit, vegetable and flower garden, now with heated greenhouses, was relocated near the stables and out of sight of the house, so as not to disturb the pastoral peace or bring even a hint of economic reality into the picture.

Mrs Pendarves, a widow who was later to become the wife of Dean Patrick Delany, was a seminal figure in Irish gardening, dancing through the pages of history both literally and metaphorically. As a young widow in the 1730s she visited Ireland for the first time, staying up dancing every night – sometimes until two in the morning. Her letters record whom she met, where she went, and details of the houses she stayed in and the gardens she visited. She gardened, sketched, made grottoes and shell houses, painted flowers and plants, sewed and embroidered, and travelled all over the countryside. She returned to Ireland in the 1750s to marry the Dean, and became the mistress of Delville near Glasnevin. Dean Delany and Jonathan Swift (the author of *Gulliver's Travels* and Dean of St Patrick's Cathedral in Dublin) were great friends with a common interest in landscape gardening. They had been to stay with the poet Alexander Pope, whose garden at Twickenham was planted in the new informal manner. They listened to his ideas, in which he urged a return 'to the amiable simplicity of nature' as he wrote: 'Let Nature never be forgot ... Consult the Genius of the Place in all', and scorned 'the ill taste of those who are so fond of Evergreens (Particularly Yews which are the most tonsile) as to destroy the nobler Forest trees, to make way for such little ornaments as Pyramids of dark green continually repeated, not unlike a Funeral procession'. Both Deans on their return beautified their gardens in the new romantic manner, and were generous with advice to their friends.

Shortly before her marriage to the Dean, Mrs Delany had visited Richard Wesley, the 1st Lord Mornington and grandfather of the first Duke of Wellington, who had been making many improvements to his demesne at Dangan, County Meath. She was enchanted by his irregularly shaped lake of 26 acres with splendidly detailed miniature fort and several ships, one a complete man-of-war. She records, 'The ground as far as you can see every way is waving in hills and dales, and every remarkable point has either a tuft of trees, a statue, a seat, and an obelisk or a pillar.' Today the neighbouring *ferme ornée* of Larchill, which must have been copied from Dangan, is being restored, complete with its original fort in the centre of a lake, several eye-catchers including a fox's set made into a temple for the eccentric eighteenth-century owner to return to in the afterlife, rare breeds of pigs and goats, and a walled garden with statues, which contains the original shell-decorated tower.

At Belvedere in County Westmeath, the garden follies and famous 'Jealous Wall' are being mended and the planting of terraces and borders revived. The 'Jealous Wall' is a teetering stone profile of what appears to be a ruined castle with Gothic windows and jagged outline, but is in fact a brilliant pastiche one wall thick, built by the owner, the 'Wicked' Lord Belvedere, who imagined an affair between his wife and his brother who lived at Rochfort next door.

It is important to remember that gardens and parks in the eighteenth century were real-life versions of a pictorial ideal. For instance, the fashionable serpentine sheets of water at Carton, County Kildare (as painted by Thomas Roberts) were modelled on the peaceful landscape of a pastoral Arcadian painting by Claude Lorrain. And the Dargle Valley in County Wicklow shown in an engraving by the Irish landscape painter, George Barret, is a version of what they had seen in the pictures of Salvatore Rosa. These two painters had become the two great inspirers of the natural garden. Gentlemen who had been on the obligatory 'Grand Tour' in Europe and were inspired by the

*Top:* The Sheet of Water *at Carton, Co. Kildare, by Thomas Roberts c.1770. Private Collection.*

*Above:* The Dargle Valley, *an engraving by Georger Barret c.1755*

*Top:* The cottage ornée *at Woodstock,*
*Co. Kilkenny, by Maria Spillsbury Taylor.*
*(National Gallery of Ireland)*

*Above: The thatched arbour at Glengariff*
*Castle, Co. Cork, c.1820. Artist unknown.*
*(Private collection)*

Italian countryside returned home with the actual pictures in their baggage
so that they could use them as blueprints for their gardens. The setting of
the Mussenden Temple, erected by Lord Bristol in his demesne at Downhill,
County Londonderry (where there is now also a charming garden), is closely
modelled on the painting by Claude Lorrain known as 'Parnassus'. In both
the painting and the garden, a domed and circular temple is perched on the
edge of a steep cliff at the bottom of which stretches an endless sea. Irish
followers of Launcelot 'Capability' Brown laid out belts of trees around the
outer perimeter, sweeping lawns, ha-has, clumps and groves of trees and lakes,
with driveways meandering through parks. Everything was planned to give
different views of the house, with huge feats of engineering being involved in
creating these 'natural' landscapes. Parks were normally enclosed within walls,
not just to keep people out, but also to provide employment in times of
hardship – garden activity in the eighteenth and nineteenth centuries often
went together with periods of famine.

In the nineteenth century, formality returned once again to Irish
gardening. The century was dominated by horticultural advances and wooden
packing cases filled with plants, which arrived from the Argentine, California,
Mexico, the Himalayas, China and Australasia. The new Botanic Gardens
in Belfast, Cork and Dublin propagated the plants and then shared them
with other keen gardeners around the country. Lilies, orchids, rhododendrons
and cacti were among the spectacular plants first introduced through Ireland
to gardens all over the world.

One of the great features of Victorian gardens was their dazzlingly
beautiful and intricate heated greenhouses. Many of them were constructed
by Richard Turner of the Hammersmith Iron Foundry, Dublin, including
those in the Botanic Gardens at Kew, Belfast and Glasnevin, Dublin. It is still
possible to find these narrow-paned, curvilinear soaring beauties hanging by a
thread, like the magnificent one joined on to the house at Ballyfin, in County
Laois, and the one in the walled garden miles from the house at Clonyn
Castle, outside Mullingar, County Westmeath, or at Marlfield in County
Tipperary. To see an enormous 1890s range of glass-houses one must study
old photographs of Kylemore Castle in County Galway, which was designed
by J.F.Fuller for the Manchester industrialist Mitchell Henry. The garden
is being restored and it is hoped that the great greenhouses will rise again.

The Great Gardens of Ireland Restoration Programme, funded by the
European Regional Development Fund, in which grants are given on
a matched basis with the owners in return for the gardens being open to
the public, has undertaken the restoration of many of these Victorian and
Edwardian gardens as well as earlier ones. Among them are the nineteenth-
century gardens laid out by C.R.Cockerell at Loughcrew in County
Westmeath in the middle of a wild and romantic demesne near the burial
cairns of pre-Celtic chiefs. The gardens at Bantry House overlooking Bantry
Bay in County Cork and the extraordinary demesne and ruined garden at
Woodstock, County Kilkenny, with free-standing circular Turner conservatory,

avenue of monkey puzzles, tepidarium, parterre, and *cottage ornée* on a wooded precipice not far from the one at Kilfane, are two more of the gardens being restored in this programme.

The gardens at Tullynally Castle, County Westmeath, are open to the public, with grotto, walled garden, herbaceous borders, Victorian summerhouse, pond with 'weeping-pillar' fountain and lake with black swans. There are stands of magnificent trees and a woodland walk planted with groups of unusual shrubs from China collected and grown from seed by the present owner, Thomas Pakenham, which surround an enamel-red Chinese pavilion. Many of the formal gardens and vistas laid out by Lady Ardilaun at Ashford Castle, Cong, County Galway, still exist, with the spray from the great *jet d'eau* blowing in the wind as it falls into the huge stone circular pond on the lough side of the famous castle hotel. Perhaps the only Victorian garden with thousands of bedding-out plants still maintained and changed twice annually is at Powerscourt, County Wicklow. Here the seventh Viscount Powerscourt plundered the gardens of Italy, France and Austria for inspiration and created a dramatic amphitheatre, with large round pond and central fountain reached by flights of steps and descending terraces with statues, urns and parterres, using the wooded valley and Sugarloaf Mountain as a backdrop.

*Above: Original watercolour by George Miller which was the source for the reconstruction of the* cottage ornée *at Kilfane, Co. Kilkenny. (Royal Society of Antiquaries of Ireland)*

*Above: A view through the wrought iron gate of a pond and fountain ringed by metal tortoises, inside the walled enclosure designed by Sir Edwin Lutyens at Heywood, Co. Laios.*

By the beginning of the twentieth century, the Victorian straitjacket that had held the natural shapes of plants and trees in check for so long was loosened by a concerted barrage of writing from the irrepressible William Robinson. His book *The Wild Garden* (1870) suggested that plants should be allowed to grow in a garden as if they were in the wild, a revolutionary idea in an epoch which had favoured the planting of forced hothouse annuals in geometric patterns. Robinson had grown up in Ireland and had gained some of his inspiration from the wilder gardens of his native land. He believed that shrubs and plants should be allowed to grow to their full size, and that native plants should be allowed to mix with the ever-increasing riot of exotic species that were being sent back to Ireland and England by the great plant-hunters. He thought that if they were all planted together as if they had happened naturally, it would give the impression of a Garden of Eden, which he believed suited the flowing landscape of Ireland. He popularized the use of hardy perennials in garden design and encouraged old-fashioned garden flowers like hollyhocks, sunflowers, lilies and roses.

On the heels of the discoveries of the Irish customs officer and plant collector Dr Augustine Henry, and with the help of Sir Frederick Moore, the director of the Botanic Gardens at Glasnevin, a flood of exhilarating hardy species began to reach Ireland from China and the remote mountains of Tibet and Burma. These flourished in the Irish climate and nurseries propagated and sold them. The Daisy Hill Nursery at Newry, the Slieve Donard Nursery at Newcastle and Watson's Nursery in Dublin set standards of excellence, while the nursery at Lissadell, in County Sligo, stocked an impressive collection of alpines, with the result that alpine gardening flourished in different rock gardens all over the country. Colonel Hill Walker even started a Japanese garden in Tully, County Kildare, which still exists today.

Perhaps one of the most fruitful combinations of talents in the history of gardening was that of the architect Sir Edwin Lutyens, and the gardener Miss Gertrude Jekyll. The gardens at Heywood in County Laois are a splendid example of their collaboration and, even though the house has gone, the eighteenth-century buildings and waterworks in the picturesque valley are being restored, and the great stone drum, pergola and terraces, with fountain and *oeil de boeuf* windows built by Lutyens looking out over the landscape, remain unforgettable. It is to be hoped that the new planting plans drawn up by Graham Stuart Thomas in the style of Gertrude Jekyll, with carefully annotated border plans as a guide, will soon be restored.

Lord Talbot de Malahide, who died in 1976, was arguably the most knowledgeable Irish gardener of his time. He built up an extraordinary collection at Malahide Castle, specializing in plants from Australasia and South America. The gardens, looked after today by Fingal County Council, still contain many of his discoveries. The Edwardian herbaceous borders at Killmurry in County Kilkenny have been recorded for posterity by Mildred Anne Butler, whose paintings recreate the atmosphere of those forgotten Irish walled gardens in the sunny afternoons before the First World War. That world of privileged security has vanished and it is only now that garden archaeologists are beginning to take seriously what it contained.

So many old Irish plants have disappeared that it is important that the gardeners of today should be encouraged to grow and propagate Irish varieties. Such a fragile part of Ireland's heritage must not be lost or the memories forgotten of those who were born or worked in Ireland, and whose gardens may have been swept away but whose names live on in the plants they discovered and saved. The interest in gardens today has broken through all boundaries, social, political and religious. Fascinating new gardens are being made all over the country. The number of garden centres is burgeoning, and there are magazines and television programmes, and an excitement about garden visiting that has never been there before. Garden and landscape design are once more career options, and the history of gardening is taught at universities, while the National Botanic Gardens at Glasnevin give student botanists and gardeners an excellent training. I raise my glass to the ladies and gentlemen, especially expert plantsmen and plantswomen like Betty Farquhar, David Shackleton, Lady Moore, and Lord Talbot de Malahide, without whom this revolution would not have been possible, and who have kept the threads of Irish gardening knowledge alive to hand on to the coming generation.

*Below: The restored vegetable and herb garden at Hilton Park, Co. Monaghan with the house in the background in which lives Lucy Madden, one of the best cooks in Ireland. She and her husband Johnny grow their own produce to cook and serve to the visitors who come to stay.*

# ALTAMONT
## COUNTY CARLOW

Altamont is situated in a remote place, hidden within the many winding lanes of County Carlow. After a sharp bend, you are confronted by a classical stone gateway of rusticated pillars topped with large stone balls supported by thin, curving stone necks, with two smaller gates on either side for pedestrians. On the other side of the gates a golden beech avenue tempts you in. Cows graze in the field beyond and, at the end of the day, rooks can be seen flying through the trees before going to roost.
A collection of rare young rowan trees is planted up either side of the avenue in the protective shade of ancient beech trees.

Altamont became a legend in the lifetime of Mrs Corona North, who owned the estate until her death in 1999, and is the result of her and her father's continuous work and attention. Often, her elegant wolfhound could be seen sitting languidly on the front steps of the old house, as silkies and bantams stalked on the gravel driveway.

*Previous page, main picture: The elegant
trunks of the beech trees in the Nun's Walk wet
with autumn rain.*

*Previous page, detail: A celtic motif based
on pre-historic carvings on the back of a seat
which stands at the New Bridge.*

*Above: Springtime is magnolia time
at Altamont.*

*Opposite above: In springtime the 100
steps lead through clumps of naturalized
old-fashioned daffodils.*

*Opposite below: This wild boulder-strewn
stream bed has the feel of the Ice Age about it.*

Indeed, for many generations of the North family there has been a close bond
with the countryside of County Carlow. Mrs North was one of the last members
of a dynasty who came to Ireland in the early 1600s, married into a local Quaker
family, and later built the nearby house of Ballydarton. They were all masters of
foxhounds, not only in Carlow but also in the Cotswolds and in Australia, and
began by starting the nearby Tullow Hunt in 1808. When Robert Gray Watson
(1821–1906), then Master of the Carlow Hunt, was told by a solicitor that he
was about to inherit Rockingham Castle in England, he replied, 'What would
I be doing with a castle in England when I have Ballydarton, and the best pack
of hounds in Ireland?' In 1923, Mrs North's parents Isobel and Fielding Lecky-
Watson rented and then bought Altamont.

Fielding Lecky-Watson was a noted plantsman, a sponsor of botanical
expeditions and a rhododendron fanatic. Therefore, when Mrs North was born,
she was called after his favourite rhododendron, 'Corona'. Over his lifetime he
bought thousands of rhododendrons, some of which he grew in his greenhouse
from seed and others he collected from abroad. Sadly, in the early 1970s many
were killed during a sharp frost, having split their bark, being vulnerable due
to a dry summer followed by a long, mild and rainy autumn. The remaining
rhododendrons are now back in force due to Mrs North's diligent replanting.

The earliest parts of the garden date back to the eighteenth century. However, most of the structure that we see today dates from the 1850s, when the Borrer family bought the demesne on the banks of the River Slaney. Thanks to the mass employment scheme in the post-Famine era, they were able to employ 100 men with horses and carts to dig out the 2½ acre lake which became the central focus of the garden. On returning from England, where she worked in the Forces during the Second World War, Mrs North found that the garden had become so overgrown that no one had been able to get round the lake for seven years. It took several years of determined hard work to clear the lake of weeds, and move and save the rhododendrons around it. From spring to autumn she toiled away in a flat-bottomed barge, moving and saving the rhododendrons, with the help of just one old man.

Mrs North was always a keen planter of trees – she often used to travel abroad with the International Dendrology Society – and they are one of the glories of the demesne. When her father died in 1943, she returned to Altamont for good with her new husband and moved into the Keeper's Cottage. Here she made a charming garden and started the Arboretum with the seeds she had collected on a trip to South America. When she had begun planting trees in her twenties, her enthusiasm had been considered eccentric, but Lady Moore, the wife of Sir Frederick Moore, director of the National Botanic Gardens, a noted plantswoman herself, had been delighted to discover the young Corona planting a noble fir (*Abies procera*) and had encouraged her interest. In the parkland of the demesne, the branches of the old chestnuts and limes reach down to the ground and outside the bowfront of the house stands a pair of nineteenth-century weeping ashes.

On her mother's death aged 102 in 1986, Mrs North moved back into the main house. The changes included making the drawing room into one room again and installing central heating. She also began to bake her own bread and make butter and yoghurt from the creamy milk produced by her herd of Jersey cows. Mrs North was a statuesque figure with turquoise-blue eyes. She had an enormous amount of energy and was immensely hospitable. In the summer it was rare to be able to reach her on the telephone until she stopped mowing late in the evening. The residential painting and gardening courses that she ran were extremely popular. She personally conducted tours of the gardens and would arrange delicious teas and cold lunches for visitors.

Against the west wing of the house, a fine *Rhododendron augustinii* (named after Augustine Henry, the famous Irish plant collector), planted by Fielding Lecky-Watson, still flourishes at 10m (35ft) tall, its gnarled old stems still producing a prolific quantity of lavender-blue flowers each spring. Old peonies grow at its feet. In the shelter of the house, a *Magnolia x soulangeana* 'Alba' thrives near the *Eucryphia lucida* as well as *Cornus kousa* hybrids, such as 'Madame Butterfly', 'Norman Hadden' and 'China Girl', with its green flowers and white bracts. Nearby, a *Clerodendrum trichotomum* with scented white flowers, which Mrs North grew from a cutting given to her by the late Lord Rosse from Birr Castle in the 1950s, is still in its prime.

From the house, a long Broad Walk edged in boxwood and punctuated by Irish yews leads under an arch of golden yew to the glassy water of the lily-clotted lake. The circumferences of the 1850 Irish yews are now all restrained by corsets of string and all of them are clipped into wonderful egg-shaped domes. The walk is bordered with old-fashioned roses such as 'Madame Hardy', 'Madame Isaac Pereire' and Mrs North's favourite 'Céleste', with its shell-pink flowers and blue-grey leaves. For spring colour, the roses are underplanted with 40 different varieties of snowdrops, several groups of the luminously yellow *Narcissus* 'Hawera' and different-coloured tulips.

*Below: Formal and informal elements are carefully blended beside the picturesque lake at Altamont.*

The lake and its surroundings are reminiscent of a painted theatre background by Oliver Messel, with the actors poised to come on stage. As you walk around the margin, two rusty swamp cypresses frame a view. Red maples glow in the wood among a forest of rhododendrons, with the original *Rhododendron* 'Corona' still there next to 'White Pearl', and in the evening a mist falls on the lake and swans dip their necks into the inky water.

Among the collection of low-growing conifers in the beds around the edges of the lake is *Pinus sylvestris* 'Hibernia', which makes an interesting small grey-blue dome. Another noteworthy plant is the primrose 'Guinevere',

*Top: The Californian tree poppy (Romneya coulteri).*

*Above: Making Altamont more than a flower garden, Corona North grew fruits of many kinds, including the delicious sweet wineberry.*

which was bred in Ireland in the 1930s. It has bronze leaves and pink flowers with a lemon-coloured eye and, because of its good constitution, it is still thriving many years after other primroses have disappeared.

The huge expanse of sloping lawn on the other side of the lake is framed by giant trees, such as a many-stemmed *Thuja plicata* on a carpet of *Anemone blanda* and *Puschkinia*, a Deodar cedar and a fern-leaved beech. By the lake stands a tulip tree (*Liriodendron tulipifera*) and a Handkerchief Tree (*Davidia involucrata*), with pure white handkerchiefs, among the first trees Mrs North planted. There are unexpected views everywhere. 'I like making vistas all over the place leading from one picture to another,' she explained, 'but this sends people who like great panoramas completely mad.' The three islands on the lake are thickly planted – pampas grass and New Zealand flax provide the architectural element among the waterside plantings of candelabra primulas, fair-maids-of-France (*Ranunculus aconitifolius*), lilies, hostas, foxgloves and dicentra.

Setting off beyond the lake through the Myshall Gate through groups of birches, southern beech and the scarlet Chilean fire-bush, you come to a Bog Garden almost swamped by the huge leaves of the giant Chilean rhubarb (*Gunnera manicata*). From here the stream flows through an Ice Age Glen, where thousands of years ago great boulders came to rest. There is a gap in the trees, where the stream unexpectedly becomes a waterfall, crashing hundreds of feet down into the River Slaney. Suddenly you are out into the clearing with the great wide sweep of river and wild, untouched woods on either side stretching ahead in an almost medieval landscape. Here, as elsewhere, Mrs North has taken advantage of every inch of scenery, with each twist and turn used to advantage in a subtle and intoxicating combination of surprises. Walking along the riverbank, you come to a staircase of 100 steps built into the steep hill of woodland. After walking up the dark staircase, through tunnels cut in the laurel thickets on the hillside, it is a welcome contrast to be led onto a high, open clearing surrounded by the green fields of County Carlow filled with sheep. Looking back from the High Ridges Walk, you can see the dense, confining woods. Ahead of you in the distance are the Blackstairs Mountains, crowned by the gentle peak of Mount Leinster.

Many of the trees at Altamont have interesting and personal histories. On the way back to the lake, you pass a giant redwood, or Wellingtonia (*Sequoiadendron giganteum*), belatedly planted to commemorate the Duke of Wellington's victory at the Battle of Waterloo of 1815 – it used to be surrounded rather picturesquely and appositely by a crown of Portuguese laurel. A balsam poplar (*Populus balsamifera*), now 35m (100ft) tall, was brought back in Mrs North's washbag from Dame Flora MacLeod in the Scottish Isle of Skye, and the storm-battered but still lovely *Prunus* 'Ukon' with its creamy green flowers was planted 50 years ago by Mrs North's father. The nuns who lived at Altamont in the seventeenth century are commemorated in an avenue of towering beech trees called the Nuns' Walk, which runs along the whole of one side of the garden, carpeted in turn through the seasons with periwinkles, lent lilies and autumn-flowering cyclamen. Walking under the thick canopy of trees, you turn right past a clipped boxwood hedge and are suddenly confronted again by the pink house hung with creepers and a pair of doves more often than not sitting on the roof. Here in a side courtyard a 150-year-old sweet-smelling climbing rose 'Blush Noisette' supports the deep blue *Clematis* 'Lasurstern'.

To one side of the house is the Walled Garden, in which an ornamental herb and vegetable garden flourishes. In one of the two greenhouses, 'Black Hamburgh' vines have been producing small sweet grapes for 150 years. There are also displays of the many varieties of the shrubs and trees in the gardens, all of which are for sale alongside delicious cakes and restorative tea.

The word 'magical' is often used to describe the atmosphere of this garden, although the endeavour that has gone into keeping it is purely human. If it had not been for the single-minded determination, skill and energy of Corona North it would not be what it is today. She formed the Altamont Garden Trust to preserve this uniquely beautiful Irish demesne with its many thousands of plants and abundance of wildlife, and to save it from the bulldozers which have been the fate of so many Irish gardens. Now, following her death it passes to the care of Dúchas, the Heritage Service of the Department of Arts, Heritage, Gaeltacht and the Islands. My generation and that of my children owe her a tremendous debt of thanks.

*Above: Orange pot marigolds, variegated nasturtiums, cabbages and herbs, including purple sage and fennel, can provide just as colourful a garden as more exotic plants. Everything in the formal potager is edible, including the tall artichokes which have been allowed to blossom.*

*Plan of Altamont*

1. Walled Garden
2. Potager & Herb Garden
3. Nun's Walk
4. Celtic Motif
5. New Bridge
6. Temple Folly
7. High Ridges Walk
8. River Slaney & 100 steps
9. Sunset Field
10. Ice Age Glen
11. Boulder Strewn Stream
12. Bog Garden
13. New Arboretum
14. Lake
15. Iron Bridge
16. Broad Walk

# ANNES GROVE

## COUNTY CORK

The square, eighteenth-century house of Annes Grove is all but buried in the lush growth of creepers. Wands of kiwi fruit cascade over the windows and at its back, the ground falls sharply away in terraces to the river.

Annes Grove was brought to public attention in 1776 by Arthur Young in his *Tour of Ireland*. In fact, it was the only garden mentioned and it was noted that the estate was rented at the time by the Aldworth family. 'Mrs Aldworth', writes Arthur Young approvingly, 'has ornamented a beautiful glen, which winds behind the house, in a manner that does honour to her taste; she has traced her paths so as to command all the beauties of rock, wood and a sweet river which glides beneath both; it is a most agreeable scenery.' The same could be said today, but the eighteenth-century vista must have shown the river against the bare gorge of the limestone cliffs which are now covered with shrubs and trees – a patchwork of greens until the autumn months when it changes to magnificent bronzes and golds.

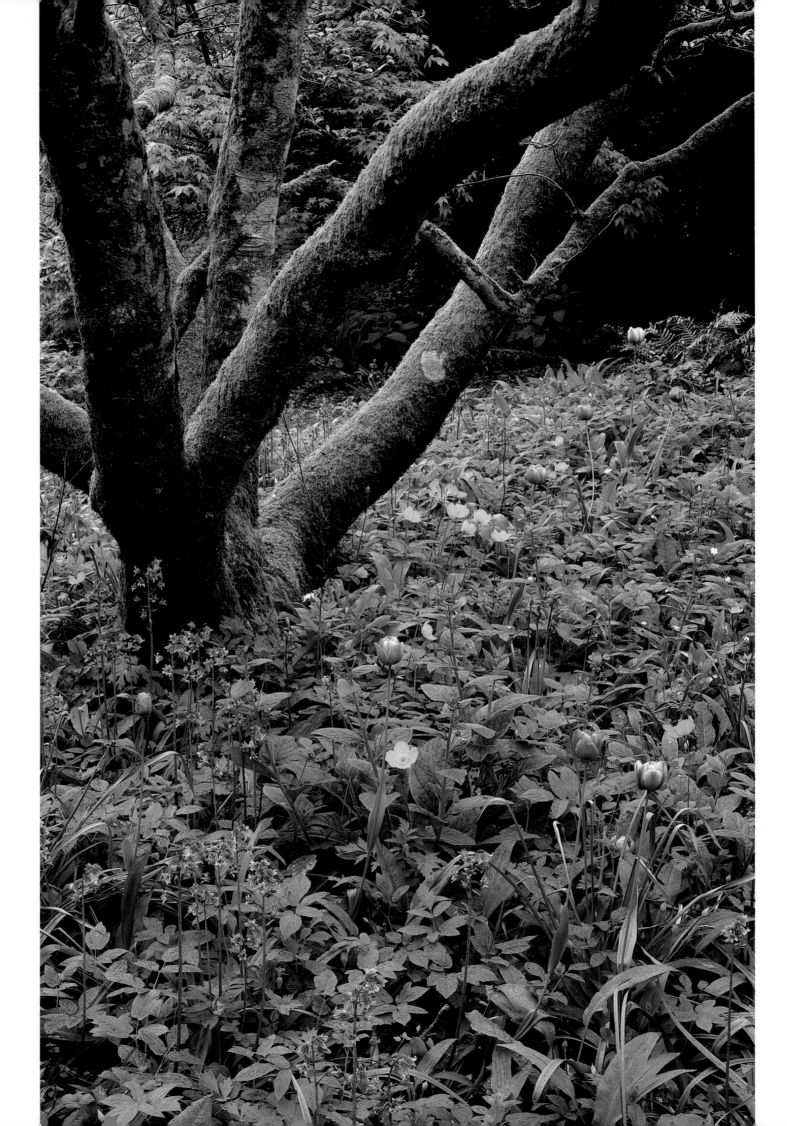

Inheriting a famous and beautiful garden created by your grandfather is a challenge, but, with the voices of his ancestors ringing in his ears, one that Patrick Annesley welcomed. In 1973 Patrick gave up his career as a publisher in London to return with his wife Jane to Annes Grove to look after the garden and to bring up their children in the family home.

The property had belonged to the Grove family since the seventeenth century. In 1764, Mary Grove, the heiress, married Francis, soon to be the 1st Earl Annesley, who built the house and later rented it to Mrs Aldworth. The Annesleys were childless, so the estate passed to their nephew Arthur, who called himself Grove Annesley. It was Arthur's son, Richard, who Victorianized the Walled Garden in the 1860s, adding colourful flowerbeds full of delphiniums and building a viewing mound. He packed the ribbon beds of boxwood with slipperworts and polyanthus, and also planted the yew walk.

Richard Grove Annesley's son, named after his father, inherited Annes Grove in 1907. He had developed a keen interest in gardening and had many connections in the Irish gardening community, including his cousin, Earl Annesley of Castlewellan, County Down (which is now the National Arboretum), Hugh Armytage Moore of Rowallane, Gerard Leigh White of Bantry House, the Bryces of Illnacullin and Sir Frederick and Lady Moore of the Botanic Gardens at Glasnevin. It is Richard who is said to have encouraged the trees and plants on the cliffs to grow by standing in front of the rock and firing seeds with his catapult into the cracks!

There was a 12 year hiatus at the beginning of the century. Richard served with the North Irish Horse during the First World War, and subsequent troubles in Ireland prevented him from gardening. After this Richard returned to his gardening with increased vigour. Before the war he had snapped up the opportunity to try to grow showy hybrid rhododendrons. Later, he subscribed to the first of a series of syndicates established by garden owners to sponsor the plant-hunting expeditions of Captain Frank Kingdon Ward in Burma and Tibet. Some of the hair-raising reports of these expeditions to the remote Himalayan valleys are still kept in the house at Annes Grove. Richard planted some of the rhododendron seeds brought back from the East on one of the slopes at the back of the house. They took so well that they look today as if they were growing in the wild. Planted alongside were well-known woodland exotics of that period, such as the Chilean fire-bush (*Embothrium coccineum*) and lantern bush (*Crinodendron hookerianum*) from South America, eucryphia, New Zealand daisy bushes (*Olearia*) and North American dogwoods. The Robinsonian influence is evident here in the large number of exotic species thriving alongside native flora, all growing together in glorious informality.

As you walk around the edge of the path from the house to the beginning of the shrubby walk that forms the backbone of these planted slopes, the scent of vanilla from the *Azara microphylla* 'Variegata' drifts through the air. This plant originated in the garden of one of the great Victorian characters of Irish horticulture, W.E.Gumbleton JP, of Belgrove, near Cobh, County Cork. The

*Previous page, main picture: The rampant kiwi fruit that curtains the outside of Annes Grove is a relative newcomer from China, introduced hardly a century ago. The house, twice this age, commands a view over the glen and River Awbeg around which a garden was made in the 1760s.*

*Previous page, detail: Autumn-flowering cyclamen emerging from a carpet of cedar needles.*

*Opposite: Under the moss-covered trunks of a magnolia, there is a colourful array of naturalized spring flowers, including Spanish bluebells, simple yellow Welsh poppies and a sprinkling of rose-pink tulips. This is gardening at its least stressful.*

*Below: Wild primroses provide a splash of colour under a beech tree in the spring.*

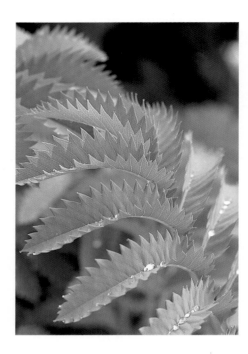

*Above: The graceful grey-green serrated foliage of* Melianthus major, *a native of South Africa that is often seen in Irish gardens.*

*Opposite: The hybrid Japanese anemone* (Anemone x hybrida) *was raised at Chiswick, England, in the middle of the nineteenth century. It is a vigorous perennial which flowers for a long period in late summer.*

showy green leaves of a catalpa and the white blossom of a self-seeded hoheria combine with the autumnal pink-tipped Persian ironwood tree and sharp spines of *Colletia hystrix* in a spectacular display. Light filters through the trees onto groups of dogwoods and the snowy-white flowers of *Cornus kousa* var. *chinensis.* The small glossy *Rhododendron* 'Blue Tit' leads to *R. falconeri* with its creamy blossoms loosely packed like Christmas bells. Pink and white azaleas and the blue *Rhododendron augustinii* are next to the scarlet 'May Day', and *R. thomsonii* has red waxy flowers with a yellow centre.

Walking towards the house from the Rhododendron Garden, you come across a rockface covered with hydrangeas whose china-blue, pink and bronze flowers tumble down to the river level. A *Magnolia macrophylla* has 60cm (2ft) long leaves, which some visitors mistake for the leaves of a banana tree. The sun falls through the branches of the sheltering pines onto the *Rhododendron sinogrande*, whose new growth resembles cos lettuce because of the silvered undersides of the leaves. The sad-looking coffin tree, *Juniperus recurva* var. *coxii* 'Castlewellan', presumably a present to Richard from his cousin, stands next to a slender peeling eucalypt and the *Rhododendron* 'Lady Chamberlain' with her very orange trumpet. A line of 300-year-old huge, tangled lime trees skirts the outside of the Walled Garden on the north side; this cuts the path and continues into the hop field which defined the boundary of the eighteenth-century garden. The Annesley silver is said to be buried beneath one of them, although treasure-seekers may be deterred by the ghost of a lady holding a flaming sword believed to drive men mad.

Descending to the river via mossy stone steps, there seem to be at least 40 shades of green on the opposite bank. The river runs beneath groves of rustling bamboo and wild meadow sweet (*Filipendula ulmaria*). Swathes of colour from the umbrella plant (*Darmera peltata*) and the autumn-pink of the katsura tree (*Cercidiphyllum japonicum*) show up against the vast dark green leaves of the ubiquitous giant rhubarb (*Gunnera*). A solitary Siberian crab apple stands next to the tallest grey poplar. Native rush and sedge, the flag iris and butterbur form a background to the candle-like Himalayan primulas and the ivory and yellow cowls of the skunk cabbages (*Lysichiton*). Water gardens had captured the imagination of the late Victorians through the paintings of the Pre-Raphaelites, and Richard used a detachment of British soldiers stationed in the nearby town of Fermoy to dig out and clear the eighteenth-century artificial canal. He changed the geometry of the old garden, remaking many of the paths down to the river and clearing the whole bank so that he could plant exotic introductions from America, the high Alps and the Himalayas, including Tibetan and Chinese poppies. He even made the river flow backwards around a little island. Rustic bridges draped in wisteria criss-cross the swirling water while, in true Monet fashion, colonies of rare water-lilies spatter the calm backwaters and tributaries of the curving River Awbeg.

Making the Himalayan climb back up the winding steps and across the path that forms the spine of the garden, you come to the Walled Garden. Following the fashions of Edwardian England, Richard Grove Annesley turned

*Left: Autumn leaves soften the contours of moss-covered steps.*

*Right: A rustic wooden bridge spanning the River Awbeg is almost hidden by the enormous leaves of the giant Chilean rhubarb which is so at home in Annes Grove.*

it into outside 'rooms' by dividing it into compartments with a series of beech and yew hedges. In one of its compartments, a curved pond is surrounded by hostas, ornamental grasses, rodgersias and other waterside plants in a way that the current owner, Patrick, thinks was deliberately made to echo the planting by the river. A twisted birch resembling a weeping willow contributes to the Japanese feel of this part of the garden, which is attributed to Patrick's grandmother. Under a magnolia, Welsh poppies, purple tulips, Solomon's seal (*Polygonatum*) and wild garlic are all planted against the heavenly blue of alkanet, which spreads outwards in a great cloud.

In another compartment, lush herbaceous borders are planted against the dark background of a yew hedge. On limestone flags from County Clare stands a sundial dated 1705. It is encased in an Arts and Crafts stone base with the words 'I only count the sunny hours' engraved on the top in Gaelic.

An avenue of enormous dark yews leads away from the rooms, forming a shady tunnel at the end of which you can see a greenhouse that has been painted white. Since the walled garden was originally an orchard, the walls facing west and south are lined with brick to retain the heat so appreciated by the fan-trained peach and nectarine trees. The tree peony 'Black Prince' has flowers the colour of the darkest red wine. Next to the late borders of purple, mauve and white Michaelmas daisies stands the Edwardian pergola, which is covered in honeysuckle, roses, vines and a delicate butter-yellow clematis.

The formal rose beds are laid out in the shape of a Celtic cross, with a mixture of Old English and Hybrid Tea roses. Clipped hedges overrun by ribbons of the red creeper *Tropaeolum speciosum* form the boundary of this compartment, and roses tumble over the outer garden walls. Both the sumptuously glossy evergreen *Clematis armandii* and *Actinidia kolomikta* climb up the wall to meet the roses. A pretty ironwork gate leads onto a cobbled track and on through another gate until you reach the main garden. As you turn away from the garden, the house comes into view from around the corner of a mass of *Rhododendron ponticum*. A carpet of pink and white cyclamen under the cedar of Lebanon lies directly across from the front door.

The back of the house is draped with clematis, roses, jasmine and white fuchsia. The dove house too is swathed with plants. One of the charming gate lodges that was on the brink of being derelict has been saved by Ireland's Landmark Trust. It has been beautifully restored and will sleep two people comfortably. Designed by Benjamin Woodward, it was the model for the gatehouse at University College Cork. It has a spiral staircase and, in the writer Mary Leland's words, 'just enough room to swing a kitten'.

It is one of life's small miracles that this eighteenth-century Irish country estate, with all its interdependent parts, still exists in a completely unspoilt state, with the original family still in residence. Nowhere else can you find a garden of such sleepy charm and beauty whose nostalgic atmosphere, far from being a mere recreation of past glories, is living proof of the dedication of its owners both past and present.

*Below: Cabbage palms from New Zealand; giant rhubarb from South America; bamboos from the Far East; all growing as William Robinson advocated – Annes Grove is an excellent example of a Robinsonian wild garden.*

*Plan of Annes Grove*

1. Walled Garden
2. Entrance in Wall
3. Oak Wood
4. Rhododendron Garden
5. Hydrangea Rock
6. Steps towards River
7. Upper Inch
8. River Awbeg
9. Island
10. Rustic Wooden Bridge
11. Front Lawn
12. Crows Walk

# ARDCARRAIG

## COUNTY GALWAY

You would never know this garden existed, hidden as it is in a lovely hazel wood. In fact, it is a series of small gardens, or enclosures, set in clearings on a windswept hillside, linked by rustic steps between different levels.

Lorna MacMahon and her late husband Harry bought the modern bungalow a short way outside Galway in 1971 in the middle of what must have seemed unpromising terrain. North-facing, with thin acid soil and little shelter from the Atlantic winds, the growing season is short and the rainfall averages a high 175cm (70in) a year. This was Lorna's ninth garden and it was a challenge she had never met before. All that existed was the boundary fences, the drive and the shell of a house. There was no soil, just rocks, gorse, heather, hazel scrub and a howling south westerly wind. However, to the north of the house Lorna had spotted a deep hollow in the front garden, in which she placed all her hope.

*Previous page, main picture: Gardens in Ireland are fortunate to be able to combine in one place so many plants of different origins, colours and textures, and then allow nature to do the rest. Lorna did plant the cowslips and the candelabra primulas, but now they seed themselves. The fountains of variegated New Zealand flax provide contrasting texture.*

*Previous page, detail: The orchid primula (Primula vialii) from Western China requires moist peaty soil. In the background are the variegated leaves of a New Zealand flax.*

Before moving to Connemara, the MacMahons had been living for five years near the Botanic Garden in Edinburgh. Here Lorna had fallen passionately in love with dwarf conifers and so one of the first things they did at Ardcarraig was to pour 34 loads of limy top soil into the front garden over the rocks to support a beech hedge and specimen trees. The dwarf conifers grew at such a rate that some have since had to be removed. The heathers and conifers, such as the golden horizontal cedar (*Cedrus deodara* 'Gold Horizon') and the upright golden yew (*Taxus baccata* 'Fastigiata Aurea') feel very much at home among the windswept Connemara hills. The weeping purple beech (*Fagus sylvatica* 'Purpurea Pendula'), on the other hand, is still only waist-high in spite of being 25 years old. With trial and error this part of the garden has achieved a sense of balance, and is now well planted with

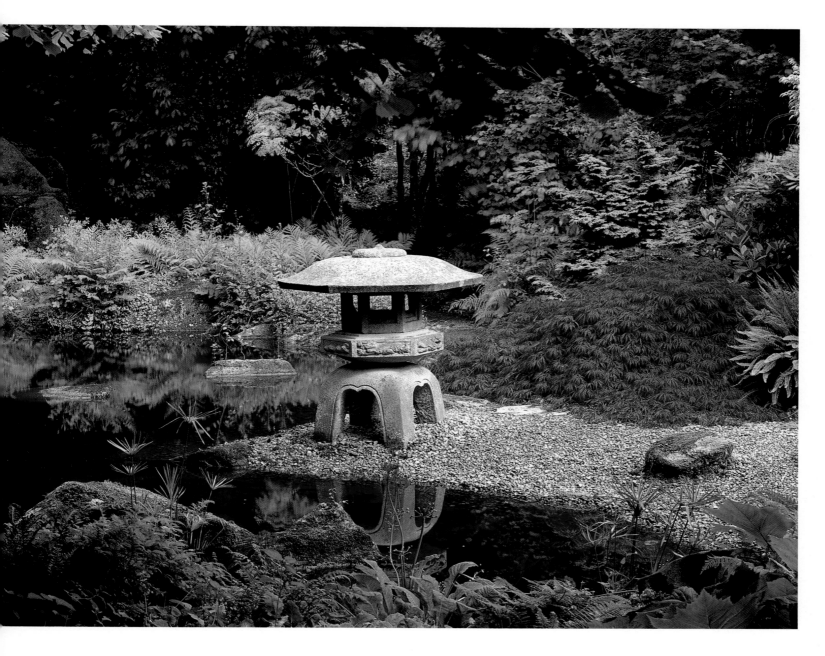

graceful taller shrubs, among which the red berries of the rowan tree and the lovely late-summer-flowering white blossoms of *Eucryphia lucida* provide a foil for the more solid shapes of the conifers. This is the quiet respectable side of the garden. 'Sweet disarray' follows in spring, when the serious-looking sharp-pinned dwarf conifers are enlivened by boisterous snowdrops and airy snowflakes (*Leucojum*), followed by riots of crocuses and daffodils.

The first enclosure you encounter when walking around the house is a formal sunken garden, planted in memory of Lorna's fanatical gardening aunts. All their favourite flowers, from *Abutilon vitifolium* to *Callistemon sieberi*, are grown around the edge of the terrace and a large Cretan terracotta pot stands in the middle as a focal point. A pergola made out of railway sleepers is covered by a lacy shawl of *Clematis tibetana* and *C. rehderiana*.

*Above left: A healthy clump of various hostas demonstrate how the climate of County Galway is ideal for gardening.*

*Above: A snow-viewing lantern with a red maple and other plants all reflected in still water conjures up visions of Japan. The triangular rock that represents Mount Fuji just happened to be in the right place.*

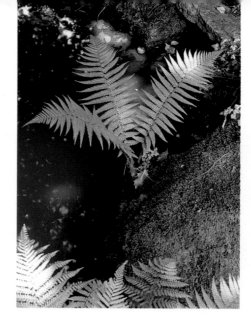

Leaving this enclosure, you walk out into the magical shadows of a hazel wood. Mosses and lichens cover the bark of trees, and glacial boulders lie scattered about, surrounded by a thick carpet of ivy and ferns. In spring, bluebells and wood anemones light up the forest floor. Hazel woods in Ireland are very precious. After the original oak woods were swept away by Neolithic farmers, the countryside was dominated by hazel woods until they, in turn, were cut down during the final woodland clearance of Tudor times. Only a few isolated pockets remain, mostly in the west of Ireland, which is why Lorna MacMahon was absolutely determined to keep as much of the hazel wood as possible, confining her gardening to the areas that had thinned out naturally, leaving only scrub, willow and bramble. Precedents for this style of garden are few: although Vita Sackville-West had made a nuttery at Sissinghurst, and nut tunnels made of hazel trees had been a formal feature of gardens for centuries, there were not many forerunners of a wild garden in a hazel wood for Lorna to copy.

The Mary O'Conor Garden is in the next clearing, created in memory of a great friend of Lorna's who, in the early 1970s, introduced a whole range of plants to County Galway via the County Galway Flower Club, including herbaceous perennials such as geraniums and unusual violas. Here you can see the blue waters of Lough Corrib over the tangle of clematis and the prolific white climbing roses 'Kiftsgate' and 'Rambling Rector' that clamber over the trees and shrubs. The branches of *Eucryphia glutinosa* and *Hoheria sextylosa* are heavy, borne down in summer with the full weight of their white flowers. From the Knight of Kerry's old garden in Valentia Island, County Kerry, comes the splendid *Myrtus luma* 'Glanleam Gold', with its orange-scented blossom and gilt-edged leaves, evoking images of Victorian brides with their bouquets of myrtle. Bright-green-leaved azaleas are tightly packed on the steep slope, while perennial cranesbills, such as *Geranium wallichianum* 'Buxton's Variety', flower in wild profusion.

The Primula Garden is packed, of course, with blue, pink and white candelabra primulas, although there are also the limpid blue flowers of the Himalayan poppy (*Meconopsis grandis*). The high rainfall during the summer months allows these to flower really well in their rocky habitat and they form large colonies in the black moorland soil in company with the purple and blue Siberian iris. Here there are also perennials, such as lily-of-the-valley, London pride and the foam flower (*Tiarella cordifolia*). The parchment-white bark of the silver birch trees is a contrast to the cinnamon-coloured trunks of the myrtles and the blood-red branches of the dogwoods. In late summer, dark blue hydrangeas and pink astilbes can just about be seen among the enormous spread of the giant Chilean rhubarb just before it collapses.

When the MacMahons bought the next piece of land, it was a complete jungle, so much so that they could hear a stream, but they could not see it anywhere. Lorna cleared away every bit of undergrowth, bush and stone so that today the sparkling stream can be seen clearly as it winds its way through what is now the Bog Garden. She had to bring all the soil and gravel in by

*Top: The moist mild climate and shelter at Ardcarraig provide ideal conditions for growing ferns.*

*Above: There are about 1200 flowering plants and ferns growing wild in Ireland which could be cultivated in gardens. Here a fern can be seen coming to life in the early part of the year, each frond unrolling like a coiled spring.*

*Opposite: Lorna has carefully retained the wild plants and ferns along the stream banks, but intermingled these with exotic poppies, primroses and hostas. The yellow tutsan (Hypericun androsaemum) is a native shrub found in wild woods throughout Ireland.*

*Above: Early summer in one of the glades at Ardcarraig. Hostas, iris and candelabra primulas weave a carpet of colour with the darker green leaves of the giant Chilean rhubarb as a backdrop.*

wheelbarrow and dig out the pool by hand to prevent the stream flooding. For the Bog Garden Lorna chose ornamental trees especially for their bark or colour of leaf, such as snakebark maples, a *Gingko*, a *Metasequoia* and different forms of cut-leaf beech. Hundreds of frogs leap through a clump of arctostaphylos. Lorna is trying to plant in every space so as to avoid using weedkiller, and lithospermum (*Lithodora*) are allowed to seed and flower in these ideal boggy conditions. Lorna has circled all the surrounding areas with holly, hazel and hawthorn to blend into the natural landscape and she has planted lobelias and day lilies, which like their feet in water. All this endeavour is quite staggering, and Lorna is very philosophical about the future: 'I have no illusions about finding anyone as cracked as I am to do what I do, but I have just had such fun and enjoyed it all so much.' She sees herself carrying on for some time yet and then, she shrugs, 'nature will take the garden back'.

The two Japanese Sections, one larger than the other, are inspired by gardens in Japan and combined with Lorna's style of gardening. For instance, 'they (the Japanese) would have clipped all the azaleas, but that would be completely against my nature,' explains Lorna. At every angle of every path, there is a new view. One particular view is of a Japanese hill and pool garden, complete with genuine snow-viewing lantern (*Uki-mi-doro*), which was brought to London, and later Ireland, by a former Thai ambassador. It is made of such solid granite and is so heavy that it would need a helicopter to move it out again. Hostas, Japanese maples, the golden form of the Japanese cedar, (*Cryptomeria japonica* 'Sekkan-sugi'), as well as *Sophora japonica* and several ravishing cherries, all encircle the lantern. A large granite rock, conveniently already in place, represents Mount Fuji and the pool is entirely surrounded by oriental plants and trees and striped Japanese ribbon grass.

In another clearing, named after her friends Mary Joe and Charlie Madden, who gave her so many unusual plants at the beginning of the garden's life, Lorna was able to nurture a number of marginally tender trees and shrubs in the sheltered and frost-free zone. Varieties of gum trees (*Eucalyptus*), pittosporum and Australian bottle-brushes (*Callistemon*) all flourish against the remains of the stony walls of what Lorna discovered were two houses that had been abandoned during the Famine.

After Harry's death in 1996, Lorna was given so many plants by friends that she determined to make a garden dedicated to him. She prepared the ground, using a pickaxe to take out all the stones, and filled up the holes with new earth mixed with mushroom compost and horse manure. She planted the hillside mostly with azaleas for spring flowers and melaleuca for colour in the summer months, with a number of low-growing Australian plants (dwarf callistemon and dwarf podocarps for example) among the granite rocks and the sheltered pools. Soon there will be magnolias here, eucryphias, lomatias, dogwoods, stewartia, lily-of-the-valley bushes (*Pieris*), rowan trees, whitebeams (*Sorbus*) and southern beeches (*Nothofagus*), all rising above the wind line and making this the most beautiful section of all in the garden.

The Herb Garden is laid out as a knot garden in raised beds and containers on the old tennis court near the house. Many of the herbs grown are old-fashioned ones, mentioned in the Bible and Shakespeare's plays, such as sage and golden hops, interspersed with hollyhocks, alliums and a little pansy called heartsease, whose other names are johnny-jump-up or love-in-idleness.

From just a small clearing back in 1971, Lorna has almost single-handedly built the unique five-acre garden – seemingly against the odds. There had long been an attitude in the west of Ireland that it was wrong to spend money and effort in planting decoratively because the area had been so deprived for so long. In addition, it was unthinkable that anyone could make a beautiful garden in such wind-swept, barren countryside, in the county to which Oliver Cromwell banished many Irish people with the cry 'to hell or to Connaught'. Lorna's skill comes in making the lie of the land work for her – and in making gardening fun. The garden gives a clear picture of its owner. Her memories of the people and places she loves are interwoven with plants and with the sites through the valley that she has cleared with such dedication. Lorna has made so intimate a mark on the landscape that the garden is as much an expression of the gardener as artist as a painting or piece of sculpture might be.

*Above: When Lorna came to Ardcarraig, this was a wild rushy place. Now she can relax, because the plants look after themselves and sometimes combine in an unexpected kaleidoscope.*

*Plan of Ardcarraig*

① Front Garden      ⑦ Stream

② Herb Garden      ⑧ First Japanese Section

③ Madden Garden      ⑨ Main Japanese Section

④ Mary O'Conor Garden      ⑩ Harry's Garden

⑤ Primula Garden      ⑪ Oak Garden

⑥ Bog Garden      ⑫ Sunken Garden

# BALLINLOUGH CASTLE
## COUNTY WESTMEATH

Lichen-encrusted eighteenth-century carved stone gate-piers opening on to empty fields in the Irish countryside are often all that remain of once prosperous estates. After the end of a family's life on an estate, the houses were sometimes burnt out or abandoned. The Land Commission would then buy the land at a nominal price and redistribute it in small acreages to neighbouring farmers. The story of Ballinlough Castle and gardens might have been one of abandonment and neglect, as after Sir Charles Nugent's in 1927 death the land was parcelled out, and the Commission was preparing to demolish the castle, when Sir Charles' grandson, Hugh, regained land and the castle back from them, and returned with Lady Nugent in 1938 to restore Ballinlough. The gate-piers that greet today's visitor are topped with urns and hung with wrought-iron gates that open onto a winding avenue. The castle sits 'on a shoulder of bright gleaming grass' against a backdrop of trees and the lake is surrounded by reeds.

*Previous page, main picture: The border of
French lavender occasionally entwined with old-
fashioned roses leads to the wooden gate that was
copied from the one at Highgrove, through which
we can glimpse the young beech hedge next to the
magnolia walk in the main walled garden.*

*Previous page, detail: Purple tufted heads
of French lavender (Lavandula stoechas).*

*Above: Pure white foxgloves (Digitalis purpurea
f. albiflora), one of Ireland's most beautiful
native flowers, will seed themselves and spread.*

*Above right: Pepe's favourite old roses with lilies
in a lavender border fill one of the smaller
walled gardens.*

Sir Hugh and Lady Nugent had the huge and complicated job of
retrieving the land and restoring the castle, gardens and woods. During the
1930s, 40s and 50s, they were able to bring the castle back to being one of
the most picturesque and varied in North Leinster, with its Gothic detailing,
curved cornices, panelled hall filled with ancestral portraits, carved staircase
and gallery, and tall rooms with beautiful mantelpieces. The gardens had
become completely overgrown and Lady Nugent put the first fork into the
ground for about 20 years in 1940. Probably her greatest achievement was to
unearth the basic pattern of the paths. Following her husband's death in
1983, she retired to live abroad, and five years later their son John and
his wife Pepe (short for Penelope) came to live here.

Today the whole garden is restored, including the Water Garden which
was rediscovered in 1940. Each compartment in the Walled Garden is like a
jewellery box filled with plants. Going away from the eighteenth-century
stabled courtyard, you pass a border filled with bluebells, hostas and Iceland
poppies and a wall with cobbled trim made from large river-washed stones.
In the Fruit Garden, cordoned and espaliered fruit trees are neatly planted,
and an octagonal fruit cage is being built to save the soft fruit from being
devoured by birds. Medlars, damsons, apples, pears, mulberries, greengages
and plums grow trained on the walls and in rows across the grass.

Two huge, colourful herbaceous borders run the length of either side of
the dividing path in the main Walled Garden. A collection of pink and yellow
epimediums flourishes near the entrance arch, and the wall at the other end
is covered by a trained wisteria, with rows of Guernsey lilies which flower in
autumn. A magnolia walk along a beech hedge leads to a Gothic gate, copied
from one in the Prince of Wales's garden at Highgrove, through which you

can see the Rose Garden. A border of French lavender leads down the centre, while old-fashioned roses line the borders along the walls with the pinks and crimsons in one corner, champagnes and creams in another.

A lovely walk can be taken from the gardens down to the canal and back through flowerbeds threaded along its banks. This area was cleared and the old rock garden dug out, and primulas, rodgersia, astilbes and crocosmia planted. Honeysuckle covers the mossy rustic stonework of the old Honeysuckle Bridge, which is made from large, irregular rocks, deliberately arranged in a seemingly random manner. It is similar to the rustic bridge at Danesmote House near Rathfarnham, County Dublin, and is also like Thomas Wright's rustic bridge at Belvedere, also in County Westmeath. Amid trees and open countryside, the canal provides a beautiful setting for the planting along the bank. A Heather Garden is being established to include the red bell heather *Erica cinerea* 'Kerry Cherry', found in the wild at Leaghillaun, County Kerry, by the late Sir Hugh.

The restoration of the gardens at Ballinlough has been aided to a large extent by a number of schemes and interested individuals. The Nugents were among the first to join the Great Gardens of Ireland Restoration Programme,

*Below: Broad, colourful herbaceous borders have been notable features of Irish gardens for the past century, so it is good to see them flourishing again in gardens like Ballinlough Castle.*

*Above: A small wooden rowing boat sits by the tranquil lake.*

*Right: Viewed from across the lake, Ballinlough Castle sits surrounded by the trees of the nineteenth century park, the walled gardens hidden from view as in many Irish gardens.*

spearheaded by Finola Reid, whereby the European Regional Development Fund provides grants to match the amount contributed by the owners of the gardens. Once the restoration is completed, the agreement is that the gardens are then opened to the public. Ursula Walsh, a student of Landscape Horticulture at University College Dublin, who was writing a thesis on the successful restoration of the historic landscape and gardens was introduced to the Nugents by Finola Reid. Ursula was so fascinated by Ballinlough that, after graduation, she accepted the post of Head Gardener and has been enthusiastically involved in the whole project ever since.

Finola says that the greatest compliment she can receive after months of work is when people say, 'But I don't see what you've been doing, it all looks just like it was.' The demesnes go back so far through Irish history and yet survive. She thinks the situation can be compared with that in Russia, the Czech Republic and other Eastern European countries. For many years it was not the done thing in Ireland to be a gardener: gardening was just for the middle class and 'elite'. Now the perception of gardening has changed and the whole country is not only middle class but also fiercely garden-minded, and all just in time to enable these magical places to be saved from oblivion.

*Plan of Ballinlough Castle*

1. Fruit Garden
2. Walled Garden
3. Rose Garden
4. Rock Bridge *c.*1820
5. Water Garden
6. Front Gates
7. Stable Yard

# BALLYMALOE COOKERY SCHOOL GARDENS
## COUNTY CORK

This garden belongs to someone who has been responsible for changing the way an entire Irish generation thinks about food, the sources of food, and the countryside. Darina and Timmy Allen are the daughter-in-law and eldest son of Myrtle Allen, who, with her fruit farmer husband Ivan, started the nearby Ballymaloe House Hotel and Restaurant in the 1960s, in their eighteenth-century house that is joined on to a medieval tower in the middle of the County Cork countryside.

Myrtle passionately believes that Irish ingredients are among the best in the world and has consistently produced the most sumptuous food in the Irish country house tradition. When she was a child, every big house and farm had its own vegetable garden and she, in turn, uses only home-grown vegetables and local produce in her cooking. Her *Ballymaloe Cookery Book* totally banished the image of Irish food being only about over-boiled cabbage and greasy chops.

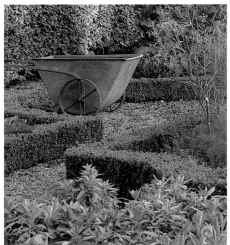

The revolution continues with Darina and Timmy, who started the Ballymaloe Cookery School in a converted farm building near their house at Kinoith in 1983. The school has expanded into the old apple store, where most of the teaching takes place, with the Garden Café and Shop next door.

An early-nineteenth-century house, Kinoith was built along the generous lines of Ireland's Regency period and is surrounded by apple orchards. The bones of the old, much smaller garden can still be seen today – it has simply expanded to meet the growing needs of both the cookery school and hotel. There are now substantial vegetable, fruit and herb gardens between its high hedges, as well as other gardens not on a strictly culinary theme, such as the Maze, the Pleasure Garden and the Herbaceous Borders. In the mid 1990s Darina secretly started work on the Shell House, which was to be a surprise twenty-fifth wedding anniversary present for Timmy.

This was also to be the focal point of an entirely new garden. The Shell House originally stood alone in the centre of an empty field. Now two straight herbaceous borders 4.5 x 100m (15 x 328ft) in length, designed by Rachel Lamb, lead away from the old garden along a green path towards the small, closed building. The beds are planted with bronze fennel, day lilies, montbretia, delphiniums, marguerites, bellflowers, violets, acanthus and mallow, all woven into a vivid tapestry. It is as if an oriental carpet has been thrown down in front of this mysterious structure which is sheltered by its scallop-shaped hedges. This part of the garden is not yet mature, but it is fascinating to see it in its early stages, reminding us that the mature gardens we see today looked like this to the people who began them, and it brings home the enormous amount of planning and hard work that goes into the carving up of a field to make a garden.

*Previous page, main picture: Cloches modelled on Victorian originals, made by Isaac, Darina and Tim's eldest son, help to ensure that this remarkable organic potager produces vegetables all the year round.*

*Previous page, detail: Withy scarecrow guarding the Kitchen Garden.*

*Above: The inspiration for the Herb Garden was Château Villandry. Like every good garden plan, the original sketch was made by Darina on the back of an envelope.*

*Opposite: Before hosepipes, this old water-barrow would have been used to fill watering cans.*

The tradition of Irish shell houses goes back to the eighteenth century to Mrs Delany and her contemporaries. There is a particularly beautiful one at Larchill in County Kildare and the famous Shell Cottage at Carton, also in County Kildare, decorated by Emily Duchess of Leinster on the death of her son, Lord Edward FitzGerald. The chaste appearance of the octagonal building at Kinoith offers no clue as to the dazzling interior within. Shells had been collected by family and friends from beaches all around the coast of Ireland and saved from the cookery school and restaurant. Charlotte Kerr-Wilson, known as Blot, an artist who specializes in shell work, came over from England to work on this secret project. With help from the Allen children, Blot began by washing the treasures she had brought with her, such as abalone shells and coral. She also suggested that the old Irish roof slates should have one end rounded off so that they looked like fish scales.

She first drew her ideas on the walls in chalk and then stuck the precious shells on top. The popularity of the seafood platter in the Ballymaloe restaurant is very much in evidence in the bands and swirls of scallops, mussels, cockles and oyster shells, while the more humble periwinkle is used as edging. Every surface is tightly covered with shells so that there is not a sliver of wall visible. The floor of the Shell House is made of pebble, and outside rivulets of pebbles have been set into the surrounding pavement. Candles are often set here in the evening.

To the right of the borders stands the Yew Maze, which was designed by Peter Lamb and Lesley Beck in a Celtic pattern and planted in 1997. The yews have not yet reached the desired impenetrability – they have a few more years' growth yet. It is fitting that there is a maze in the garden at the school as they were considered symbols of man's quest for truth and enlightenment.

Back up the path to the left of the house is the old garden, which is believed to date back to the 1840s. It is known as Lydia's Garden, after Lydia Strangman, who persuaded her father to build her a summerhouse there in 1912. The floor was laid with the ceramic chips of broken blue, white and pink kitchen china in the shape of a shamrock, rose and thistle. In 1972 this part of the old garden was totally overrun by weeds. The Allens cut back the antique beech hedge, then entangled with briars and ivy, and planted the borders around the lawns with roses and asters, penstemons and mallow, pinks and lavender, with holly and laurel for shelter. The rustic Tree House was then built beyond the little pool. From here you can see the surrounding countryside, the Herbaceous Borders that stretch to the Shell House, as well as the specimen trees and pond in the Pleasure Garden, and the Herb Garden on the other side of the high beech hedge.

Having been inspired by her visit to the potager and herb gardens at Villandry in the Loire Valley, Darina's Herb Garden contains every conceivable culinary and medicinal herb. The herbs include rosemary, thyme, blue-leaved sage, lemon balm, lemon verbena, garlic chives, tarragon, comfrey, hyssop, evening primrose, camphor, different kinds of sorrel, as well as lots

*Above: Bees enjoying the nectar from the round heads of the globe thistle.*

*Opposite: Silver and blue with a splash of orange in one of the new borders that leads you towards a mysterious small garden building.*

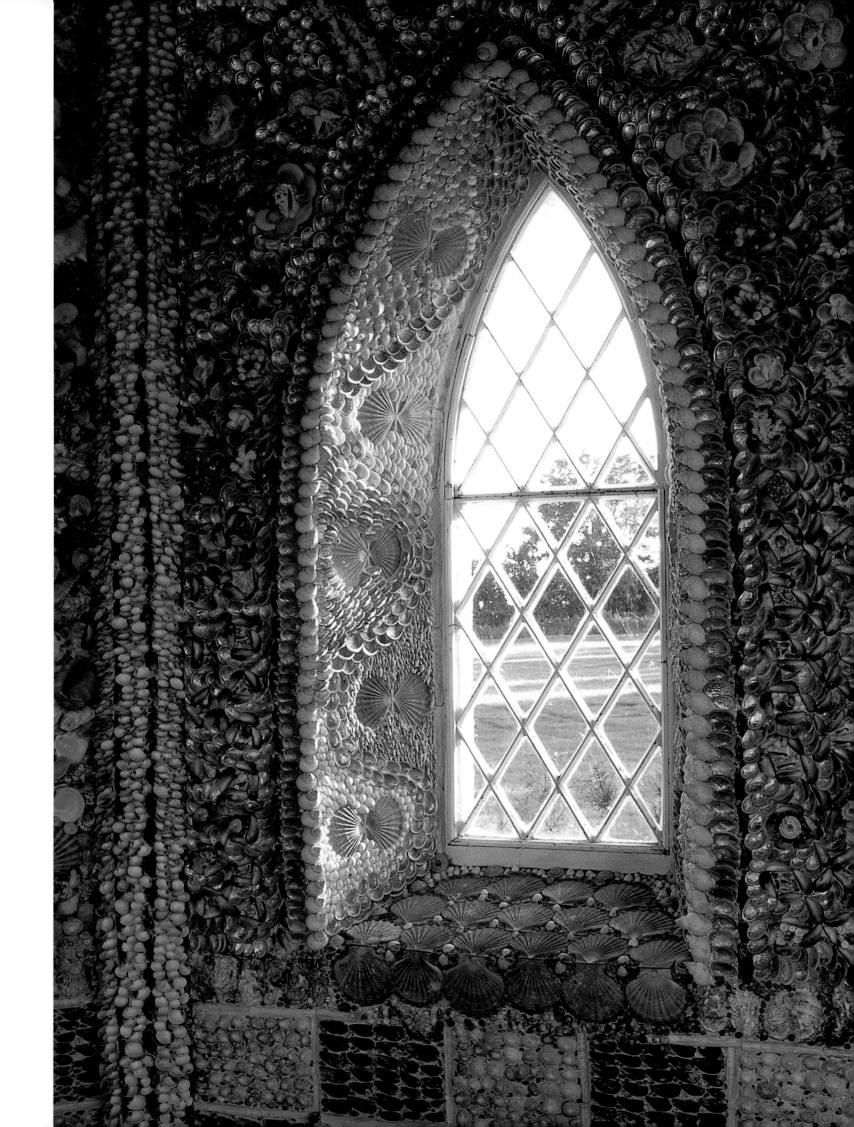

of different mints such as apple mint, ginger mint, eau-de-cologne mint and spearmint. The herbs are planted in medieval-patterned beds set among gravel and enclosed by boxwood. There is a beech exedra at one end of the plot and a gazebo at the other. Among the herbs are edible flowers, such as violas and marigolds, which are also gathered every day by students and gardeners at Ballymaloe. Also here are sea-kale plants, whose leaves are forced into succulent whiteness under terracotta pots with lids. The Herb Garden is the heart and soul of the gardens at Ballymaloe, and the part that has made the greatest impression on garden visitors over the years.

The compartment next to the Herb Garden was an impenetrable thicket before Darina cleared it away and planted a lawn with specimen trees. In spring the cherry and apple trees blossom and out come the dark red bells on the crinodendron and the fluffy scarlet flowers of the Australian bottle-brush. There is a pond, and a temple made from pillars rescued from a demolished house in Kilkenny, all sheltered by a line of ancient beech.

The Kitchen Garden was finished in 1993. The soil here is excellent since it had been used as a dump for mushroom compost for many years. It is sheltered by a little wood, and the path through this to the Kitchen Garden is always occupied by hens. Diamond-shaped boxwood parterres are filled with seasonal vegetables, and other beds are edged with frills of flowers, such as orange and yellow nasturtiums, edible marigolds and chrysanthemums, violas, cornflowers and purple catmint. Four clipped standard bay balls stand in the centre of the beds and a spiral of twisted boxwood in the middle of the herringbone brick paths. The vegetables are rotated each year within the beds according to the planned crop rotation system. An extraordinary mixture of vegetables is constantly ready each day for seasonal picking. Beans (broad, French and runner), peas, ruby chard, every sort of lettuce, spinach, Greek cress, radicchio, orach, broccoli, curly kale, pumpkins, globe artichokes, corn salad, lamb's lettuce, sweet corn, asparagus, radishes and Chinese cabbage are all grown in succession, topped by a beaming fringe of golden sunflowers at the top of the patch. Seven varieties of tomato are grown in the greenhouse.

Next to the school is the formal Fruit Garden, designed by Jim Reynolds. Against the walls are fan-trained peaches and apricots, pears, an almond tree, pink and yellow and summer and autumn fruiting raspberries, tayberries and loganberries, several mulberries, gooseberries, wine berries, and black, red and white currants, greengages, plums, an olive tree and old Irish apple trees trained over arches. These Irish varieties of apples have been rescued from old orchards and walled gardens all over the country.

This is a garden that has evolved organically and has an aura of vitality. Darina Allen is an inspiring and dedicated teacher, and with her interest in garden design it is inevitable that she will create more gardens as her plans evolve. But despite its constant evolution, this garden has not lost its connection with the past – the atmosphere of the quiet Edwardian garden that once stood behind its enclosed hedges in the middle of apple orchards is still there, but running through it is a buzz of modern excitement and purpose.

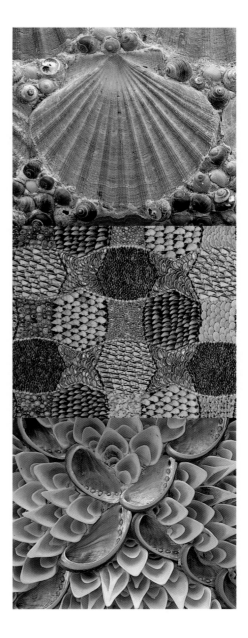

*Above: The shells that decorate the walls of the Shell House came from local beaches or from the cookery school and hotel kitchens.*

*Opposite: Roses and swirls and ribbons of shells smother the inside of the mysterious small building – Darina's inspired present for Timmy.*

*Proposed Plan of Ballymalloe Cookery School Gardens*

1. Tree house
2. Rose Garden
3. Provencal Allée
4. Shell House
5. Irish Apple Meadow
6. Maze
7. Green Garden
8. Wilderness and Pool
9. Pool and Temple
10. Pleasure Garden
11. Ornamental Fowl
12. Fruit Garden
13. Herb Garden
14. Lydia's Garden
15. Kitchen Garden

# BIRR CASTLE
## COUNTY OFFALY

The Gothic baronial pile of Birr Castle has been home to the Parsons
family, later the Earls of Rosse, since 1620. The fortified castle stands
in its 150 acre demesne in the middle of Ireland on a dramatic site perched
over the sparkling River Camcor as it flows through the wooded valley.
The roofs of the town of Birr cluster around its walls.

The gardens exude a peaceful atmosphere of tranquillity, and to wander
through them is a soothing experience. Birr is a fine example of a landscape
park with an artificial lake, and, unlike many similar landscape gardens
in Ireland, it has had a continuous programme of new planting since the
1930s. The trees are mature and the planting is so graceful that the overall
impression of the gardens is one of light and space. Over the centuries,
the castle and townspeople have always been interdependent, and over the
last three generations, members of the Parsons family have been especially
gifted and particularly knowledgeable gardeners.

*Previous page, main picture: The honeysuckle covering this stone wall is* Lonicera etrusca *'Michael Rosse', named after the present Earl of Rosse's father.*

*Previous page, detail: The remarkable sloe-coloured cones of George Forrest's fir (*Abies forrestii*).*

*Above: Elegant stone urns are ideal focal points in the Formal Gardens.*

*Above right: The* allées *of hornbeam with arched and interwoven branches are tunnels of green in midsummer.*

When the Parsons came here, having taken over the O'Carrolls fortress in the seventeenth century, there are accounts of them chopping down an orchard and buying new fruit trees. A recipe book from that time has a list of many herbal remedies, as well as a recipe for 'hartichoke pie' made from Jerusalem artichokes grown in the castle's walled kitchen gardens that still exist today.

It was Sir Laurence Parsons' grandson, the second Earl of Rosse, who gave the castle the appearance that we see today. He turned the house away from facing the town and Gothicized the front directly opposite the park. In 1810, he spanned the river with one of the earliest surviving suspension bridges. His son, William, third Earl of Rosse, became one of the most distinguished astronomers of the nineteenth century and built in Birr what was the largest reflecting telescope in the world. His wife, Mary, was a Yorkshire heiress, and it was with her fortune that he was able to carry out so many 'improvements'. In addition, he had built a series of Vaubanesque fortifications, which provided employment and relief during the Famine. Unfortunately, much of his planting went unrecorded. However, his splendid giant redwood still exists, as does the wonderful fernery planted by the countess.

The present earl's grandfather, the fifth Earl, started gardening in 1908, but only had six years at home before fighting in the First World War. By levelling a part of the moat, he and his wife Lois created the terraces built up from the river to the west of the castle. They also started the Formal Gardens and planted the first magnolias. The fifth Earl was in correspondence with Augustine Henry, the Irishman who had made collections of plants in China in the late 1880s, and who inspired his son Michael to become a botanist.

Michael, the sixth Earl of Rosse, who succeeded his father in 1918 after he was killed in action, acquired an encyclopaedic knowledge of botany. He also corresponded with Chinese botanists and organized key plant-hunting expeditions in China, including Tse-Tsun Yu's expedition to remote parts of western China. Today, many of the seedlings raised from Yu's seed are mature trees and shrubs at Birr. The archive records even reveal his 10 shillings' worth of shares in the Kingdon Ward expedition to China, with the dividend payable in seeds. Michael also collected plants and seeds on his own trips to places such as Mexico and Tibet. The result is that Birr Castle contains one of the most important collections of woody plants in Ireland, many of which were raised from seeds collected in the wild. The fact that the collections were of such scientific importance prompted Michael Rosse to invite the Heritage Gardens Committee of An Taisce (the Irish National Trust) to catalogue the trees and shrubs, a project which was undertaken by Mary Forrest with the support of the National Botanic Gardens, Glasnevin. Michael was also known for his generosity in liberally distributing plants to other Irish gardens.

*Below: Viewed through one of the 'windows' in the* allée, *pyramids and scrolls of clipped box recreate the style of gardening fashionable in the eighteenth century.*

*Above: Birr Castle stands at the end of one of the vistas through the eighteenth Century park. On the right is 'Lord Rosse's Leviathan', the great telescope.*

In 1935, he married Anne, the daughter of Leonard Messel, who had created the famous garden at Nymans in Sussex, and it was in their care that the demesne really came into its own. Messel's grandson, the present earl, remembers that one of his favourite sayings was 'a penny for a plant and a pound for the planting'. The gardens at Birr today are formally twinned with Nymans so as to ensure the continuing exchange of plants, as well as visits to each other's gardens by the head gardeners. The late Anne, Countess of Rosse, was a most intelligent gardener, with great artistic gifts, and it was really her feeling for design and her 'painterly eye' that gave rise to the sense

*Above: The lake was created by damming the River Camcor in the late eighteenth century. Wild sedge and rushes and other plants characteristic of marshy places have colonized the shoreline.*

of visual satisfaction gained from looking at the sweep of Brownian landscape down to the lake. To celebrate their marriage, she designed the pleached hornbeam cloisters edged with ribbons of snowdrops in the Formal Gardens. The square of baroque tunnels has a filigree of branches carefully espaliered and then trained to curve and entwine at the top. Cut into the leafy walls are windows through which you can see a pair of stone urns from Bavaria standing in the middle of the boxwood parterre. There are also boxwood obelisks at each corner. Statues of the Graces sheltered by rose-enclosed arbours can be seen at one end of the leafy tunnels, and the pink petals

*Top: The pure white blossoms of this magnolia stand out on leafless branches against the sparkling river Camcor and the vivid green of its' grassy river banks.*

*Above: Magnolias are one of the special attractions of Birr Castle, flowering from the beginning of spring.*

of *Magnolia* 'Michael Rosse' beckon at the other. There is a backing of thick yew hedge at one side with a border still retaining many of the original plants including yellow day lilies, peonies and an edging of catmint. Against the wall is a lush herbaceous border containing single, double and semi-double purple, white and blue delphinium hybrids, in the middle of which is the white-painted garden seat that Anne designed with their initials inter-twined to form the back. Magnolias flourish in the long grass in a row on the lawn opposite.

Walking down from the castle in the spring past the terraces and seeing a cloud of blossom ahead, it is exciting to realise that so many plants have been named after members of the family, including the magnolias 'Michael Rosse' and 'Leonard Messel', *Camellia* 'Leonard Messel', *Paeonia* 'Anne Rosse' and even a honeysuckle, *Lonicera etrusca* 'Michael Rosse'. The gardens at Birr certainly demonstrate that it is a fallacy to think that magnolias cannot be grown in lime. In fact they positively thrive, especially down by the River Camcor, where a quilt of blue-eyed Mary (*Omphalodes cappadocica*) covers the ground around their feet. Anne Rosse had found these celestial-blue flowers growing in a solid carpet under an avenue of trees in an exquisite garden in the nearby demesne of a Carolean house called Gloster. They seem to be more vigorous and healthier and have larger and bluer flowers than the forms cultivated in England, and it is thought that they could have been an old Irish cultivar, which had been 'lost' and then 'found' again. Another jewel-like Irish garden variety growing at Birr is the ravishing *Omphalodes cappadocica* 'Starry Eyes', which has a white eye in the centre of blue petals rimmed with pale mauve and a darker blue central flash.

Kowhai (*Sophora tetraptera*) from New Zealand, with its mustard-yellow blossom, spreads itself across the grey castle walls. Looking back through

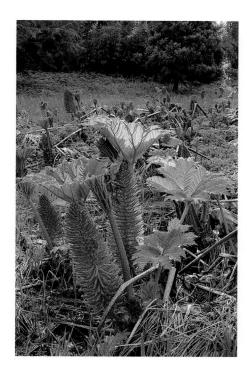

a clearing, the pink flowers of *Magnolia dawsoniana* and *M. x veitchii* stand out against the background of dark green conifers and the glittering river. A trimmed hedge of flowering quince edges the Terrace Walk, where the huge *Magnolia delavayi* with its grey-green leaves was supplied by the Veitch nursery just before the First World War. Ahead of you stands what is reputed to be the largest grey poplar in the world, with its roots stretching down towards the widening, rushing river.

In spring, hundreds of aconites and daffodils spread under the trees by the river. At the old Brick Bridge, the Little Brosna meets the River Camcor, with the lake on one side and the river on the other. Strange and mysterious sluices hidden among laurels, boxwood and wild violets are controlled by elaborate nineteenth-century machinery, and a channel of the river is tied into a clever knot and then whirled underground and out into the lake beyond. During the eighteenth century, the river used to run through the lake and it is the head race that goes under the path. A weeping willow is reflected in the water and sometimes you can see a swan swimming through the reeds. A pale pink October cherry (*Prunus subhirtella*) is planted in contrast to the holm oak (*Quercus ilex*) leaning over the bridge, and from anywhere in the park you can see the three gold willows (*Salix alba* 'Britzensis') standing next to a slash of orange barberry and the eighteenth-century beech trees.

Across the bridge, you walk through a tunnel of bamboo, so curved and with such crisp edges that it feels as if you are in a modern building. You emerge into a fairyland vista opposite the castle, with the branches of a *Magnolia kobus* framing the flowery banks across the river. In spring the giant Chilean rhubarb (*Gunnera manicata*) begins to unfold and a dark green Monterey cypress (*Cupressus macrocarpa*) stands in a field of fritillaries.

*Above: The brick bridge over the river Camcor; nearby, three counties, Tipperary, Offaly and Roscommon, meet within the demesne.*

Ducks fly upstream and the park is alight with magnolias. Looking back across the water you can see purple aubrieta stream down the high stone wall holding up the castle side of the river, with the thin suspension bridge balanced delicately from bank to bank.

Turning back and following the curve of the river past the lake, you reach a small pocket of wild woodland, followed by an avenue of young cherries. On your left is an astonishing huge flowering pear tree, which looks, in blossom, like a white cloud surrounded by seven huge mounds of very old boxwood. Leaving the lake and the Arboretum, you come to the Fernery, which the 'Telescope Earl' and his wife started work on in 1850 as the last burst of their improvements. From under the laurels you suddenly see a solid sheet of water tipping over a sharp-edged rock into a rocky gully with horny tufa walls and dribbling streams. The stream rushes down the gully and gravity fuels a hidden fountain so that the water flies up from the riverbed in three spiralling jets. Alison the present Countess of Rosse says that, when she first came to live here, this area was completely overgrown and when the Conservation Volunteers cleaned out the riverbed, they found the original blocked fountain pipes. Ferns grow up the edges of the gorge in a damp microclimate of their own, which she hopes will suit the two Australian tree ferns (*Dicksonia antarctica*) that she planted there in 1998.

Walking again towards the Formal Gardens, you can see over the wall the candles of magnolia buds in spring, and you come to the nerve centre of the demesne. Here are the greenhouses and propagating houses, which fuel all of Birr's planting. Nearby stand two thin rows of boxwood, which have grown and grown, making them, according to the *Guinness Book of Records*, the tallest boxwood hedges in the world. They would have been part of Sir Laurence Parsons' original seventeenth-century garden plan. Ancient yews, apple trees and romantic roses, such as 'Duchesse de Montebello' and 'Belle Amour', fill another walled garden, while in a small garden on the side of the greenhouses a vast twisted wisteria embraces an iron support.

Crossing the park by the Meridian Path drawn from the telescope towards the Formal Gardens, you pass the lime trees planted by the present earl and countess to commemorate the nebulae discovered by the 'Telescope Earl'. Beyond the oaks, Manchurian birch, southern beech and Turkish hazel, you come to the telescope itself, which for so long was the focus of attention throughout the scientific world. With the help of the government and the Ireland Funds, 'Lord Rosse's Leviathan' was restored in the 1990s. Around it the Great Gardens of Ireland Restoration Programme is helping to conserve and restore the gardens to their original splendour, illustrating as they do so many different aspects of the fashions and history of Irish gardening.

*Above: Springtime – a naturalized drift of daffodils on a slope beside the river with one of Birr's many magnolias.*

*Plan of Birr Castle*

1. Entrance
2. River Camcor
3. Telescope
4. Meridian Path
5. The Lake
6. Arboretum
7. Brick Bridge
8. Fernery
9. Kitchen Walk
10. Formal Gardens
11. Yew Avenue
12. Orchard

# BUTTERSTREAM
## COUNTY MEATH

The creation of Butterstream did not follow the conventional Irish formula of grand house and grand garden, with parks, lodges, follies and grottoes. The owner, Jim Reynolds, had always wanted to have a garden, but, beset by images of traditional demesnes in the surrounding countryside, he couldn't quite see how a garden could work as an entity of its own without the accompanying impressive house. And then, as an archaeology student, he visited Sissinghurst and everything fell into place. Here at last was a garden that didn't follow the norm: rather, Italian Renaissance meets the English countryside, the only building in sight being a Tudor gate-house. And yet the enclosures, paths, hedges, borders, terraces and trees all had a life and a logic of their own within the structure of the garden itself. Vita Sackville-West and her husband Harold Nicolson had created a garden out of a wilderness – and so could Jim. Life on the Reynolds' family farm in Trim, County Meath, would never be the same again.

*Previous page, main picture: At the base of the tower inspired by a local ruined pigion house grow good old-fashioned cottage garden plants; delphiniums, phloxes, double white sneezewort and campanulas.*

*Previous page, detail: View from the tower.*

Jim didn't have much to work with. On one side of the road, there was the busy town of Trim, and on the other a field. And that single field formed the basis of the magical gardens we see today. Armed with spade, shovel, saw and sledge-hammer, Jim single-handedly set to work in 1970. He began by fencing off a little bit of the land and planting a beech hedge. The first major task was to drain the relatively low-lying old flood plain, which was traversed by a stream *en route* to the River Boyne. The banks had to be levelled, scrubby hedges dug out, and several farm buildings removed.

Working by now as an archaeologist for the Office of Public Works during the day, Jim gardened in the evenings and at the weekends. He thought big, and visited gardens all over Europe looking for inspiration, starting in Ireland with Birr Castle, Illnacullin and Mount Stewart. He devoured garden books that came his way, especially ones by his heroine Vita Sackville-West and heroes Lanning Roper and Graham Stuart Thomas. What had started as 'an irrational urge to possess a few roses' developed over the years as he implemented the principles of design, layout and planting. As his plans became more ambitious, so the parameters of the field widened. 'Most of my knowledge', he sighs, 'has come, expensively, through experience.'

As the garden took shape, Jim began to develop a name for himself within the gardening fraternity, and came to the attention of the general public after Sybil Connolly and Helen Dillon included the garden in their book, *In an Irish Garden* in 1986. Since then, Butterstream has become one of the most admired of all modern Irish gardens. Jim wrote a gardening column for the *Irish Times* and lectures. He also makes television appearances and crisscrosses the county offering advice on garden design and planting. He is chairman of the Great Gardens of Ireland Restoration Programme, where his enormous enthusiasm and knowledge are constantly called upon to encourage others. Having visited the gardens of Ireland's mild coastal region, Jim,

*Above left: View of the Italian Garden with pond and temple. The rose 'Belvedere Rambler' looking like a pale pink powder puff, climbs the small square building which came from the late Georgian gate house at Grangemore in County Westmeath and which Jim bought for a song in 1985.*

*Above: This is the Italian Garden viewed from the other side of the Liscannor flagged terrace showing the 5 balls of boxwood in their earthenware pots. The pool is filled with water lilies.*

*Above: The dark double-flowered opium poppy comes out in June and, along with peonies and columbines, is one of the early delights of the herbaceous border.*

perhaps naively, assumed that he too could grow camellias, rhododendrons, Chilean fire-bushes and all the other Robinsonian delights. He soon learned that the heavy limestone soil and hard winter frosts of the midlands of Ireland are not suitable for what he originally had in mind. So he turned his attention to roses. They are one of the abounding delights of Butterstream. They are given the utmost freedom and, as a result, are everywhere you look, blurring the strict geometry of the layout of the garden. Jim's passion is for the scented old hybrid musk and species roses. He describes the 'Jacques Cartier' rose as being pink and full, opening out flat with an enfolded centre. The 'Ferdinand Pichard' rose is a striped pink Bourbon rose, which Vita Sackville-West said was like the 'finest claret stirred into whipped cream'. 'Madame Hardy' is a lovely flat white rose with a green eye, and 'Céleste' is loose and a delicate shell pink, which has the most exquisitely formed small buds of all. 'Madame Alfred Carrière' is a vigorous white climber with a hint of green in her large

*Above: The massed seed pods of the poppies are
as handsome as the flowers and provide tints
of blue and grey. Pale toadflax and tall dark
alliums add to this inspired arrangement.*

flowers – 'she hurls herself over everything'. The delicious pink-cupped
'Belvedere', which was named after Anne, Countess of Rosse found it growing
in the garden at Belvedere House, on the shore of Lough Ennell, outside
Mullingar, County Westmeath; it can grow to 12m (40ft). Graham Stuart
Thomas records seeing one cascading out of a holly at Nymans in Sussex,
where it had been grown from a cutting brought over from Ireland.

The entrance to Butterstream, opposite a housing estate, is quietly
nformal. A bower of roses marks the beginning of the garden and gives a
cottagey feel. From here, a winding path leads, in spring, through snowdrops
and crocuses and hellebores and pulmonaria, small trees, shrubs and species
roses. This is the romantic end of the garden, with a little gothic bridge
leading to a trellis topped with a gilded pineapple. As well as giving the roses,
and a *Clematis macropetala* support, Jim thinks that this construction looks
back to past glories. Among the roses is the stunning shell-pink rose 'Souvenir

*Above: Formality is achieved by tightly clipped box hedges and gravel paths as well as the carefully positioned pots of marguerites. This is the White Garden which lies below the tower.*

de St Anne's', named after Lady Ardilaun's garden in Dublin, at the foot of which is a forest of opium poppies, foxgloves, alliums, toadflax, self-seeding feverfew and cranesbills. Ground cover of ferns and the pretty candelabra primrose 'Lissadell Pink', which was raised in the nursery at Lissadell in the 1930s, gives way to edgings of rippling green hostas as you approach the stream. Jim firmly believes that gardening should be a relaxing pursuit and urges you not to worry that you haven't sprayed the roses, or that the slugs are eating the hostas. Rather, he says, nature can't always be pristine and shining, and you should look up rather than down on the garden tour.

The walls of the outdoor 'rooms' are made of hedges, which provide shelter from the cold in winter and protection from the drying winds that cross the steppes of County Meath in summer. The original three rooms have expanded to a total of 15, with a collection of connecting anterooms, corridors and stairways. Each room acts as a showcase for its own particular garden idea, and yet all lock together in perfect synchronicity. The lines have been meticulously drawn and the wild nature of plants taken into account.

The Green Walk, flanked by contrasting foliage, leads to the enclosure filled, seasonally, with hot oranges and reds through to bronzes and gold. The scarlet *Dahlia* 'Bishop of Llandaff', red and yellow tulips and orange oriental poppies, the fiery red *Crocosmia* 'Lucifer', the golden false acacia (*Robinia pseudoacacia* 'Frisia'), bronze New Zealand flaxes and a bronze cabbage-palm (*Cordyline*) sizzle together, hemmed in by a high hedge.

Walking on through a green opening, you enter another section dedicated to old-fashioned roses: Damask, Gallica, Bourbon and Moss. In midsummer, if you climb to the top of the tower inspired by a local ruined pigeon house, you look down onto a wave of crimson, pink and white roses breaking and frothing over the top of the green walls, which only just prevent them from clambering into the White Garden next door.

The White Garden is made up of four squares, divided by paths and clipped hedges. Depending on the time of year, there are bellflowers, peonies, the famous and desirable Chinese tree peony 'Joseph Rock' and lots of white tulips. White toadflax arrives early in the year, followed by *Hydrangea arborescens* 'Annabelle', many white roses, double white sneezewort (*Achillea ptarmica* 'The Pearl'), white goat's rue (*Galega*), clouds of phlox mixed with silver foliage plants and variegated grasses. Tall cardoons add height and architectural form. The main passageway is clipped in layers and down the centre run five pairs of terracotta pots filled with white marguerites sunk into the wide hedges standing on either side of the path in their own carved outer pots of boxwood. 'From up in the tower,' says Jim with satisfaction, 'you can see the very straight lines of the hedges with mad confusion inside.'

Just beyond the White Garden, you catch a glimpse of the wild profusion of the herbaceous borders. These are a series of deep beds interwoven by curving grass paths. In springtime there are lots of tulips, and then the various networks of herbaceous plants start to develop. In late Spring, there are opium poppies, peonies and columbines, mixed up with sweet rocket, and then the first delphiniums appear, accompanied by most types of bellflower – in blues, mauves and pinks – and finally the delicious little red scabious *Knautia macedonica*. In contrast to the early colours – pale yellows mixed with blues, pinks and silvers, which Jim can find 'a bit boudoirish' – the late summer sees stronger colours: the old-fashioned varieties of phlox, followed by hemp agrimony (*Eupatorium*), goat's rues, loosestrifes (*Lythrum*), lobelias and Japanese anemones. The strident yellow and purple of the two meadow rues (*Thalictrum lucidum* and *T. delavayi*) and the perennial sunflowers are set against the lovely yellow-cream herbaceous *Potentilla recta* var. *pallida*.

Leaving the herbaceous borders, you come across an elegant sundial, bought from a traveller in 1976. In this room, the white climbing rose 'Kiftsgate' grows alongside the sturdy cream-coloured 'Rambling Rector', which was first included in the Daisy Hill Nursery catalogue in 1912. The 'Sanders White Rambler' tumbles over the wall and banks of milky bellflower (*Campanula lactiflora*) are punctuated by the spikes of delphiniums.

Walking through the Laburnum Tunnel, you come to the Obelisk Garden, which Jim started after an ash tree blew down, annihilating a greenhouse. Bridget Ordway of Blackcastle had given him 14 boxwood plants, which he now clipped into little pyramids and set into gravel in a square formation,

*Top: Corners of the White Garden with marguerites in pots and milky bellflowers.*

*Above: Part of Jim's 'mad confusion' of herbaceous plants – white rosebay willowherb with masterwort, campanulas and meadow rue.*

*Above: Illusions of grandeur – the canals and pavilions were built from scratch a few years ago in what was an open field.*

adding a larger clipped obelisk in the centre. One side is his 'seven virtues' and the other side his 'seven deadly sins'. The idea for this garden came to Jim as he was lying in bed thinking of the Piranesi print of the Circus Maximus.

Across the laurel lawn, you come to the Pool Garden, an evocation of a villa garden in Pompeii, which houses a small Tuscan square temple. Lollipops of hornbeam grow in flowerpots of clipped box. Mock orange blossoms hang over the pillars of the temple and white willowherb grows beyond. There are water lilies in the pool and the rose 'Belvedere Rambler', climbs over the pergola. This compartment seems to be the end of the journey, but if you press on you find a little secret path under two old trees, which leads to an airy lawned area. Two small temples either side of the lawn are covered in winding clematis. Growing around are Musk roses, cranesbills and the mop-headed false acacia, as well as the sycamore *Acer pseudoplatanus* 'Brilliantissimum', which has leaves stained shrimp-pink and apricot in spring.

*Below: Evening light on a gothic bridge, one
of Jim Reynolds' many formal embellishments
in Butterstream.*

The stone doorway that was salvaged from an eighteenth-century house
in Trim, owned by Lord Mornington, is set into the wall that leads through
a terrace to the two pavilions built on either side. These, Jim admits, were an
act of folly, but he couldn't resist trying to capture the essence of the 1750s.
The pavilions do not block any view in the garden. From their Venetian
windows you see two canals, at the end of which grass steps lead to a pair
of seats where you can sit and contemplate the lime *allées* and holly hedge.

After a delicious tea, you then wend your way home, leaving via what Jim
calls the Vegetable Department. Peas, beans, sea kale and artichokes grow in a
formal design of a little avenue of seven high boxwood obelisks. Old-
fashioned iron arbours have Irish varieties of apples trained over them to show
off their blossom and fruit. On the way out, you might buy perhaps Lady
Ardilaun's vigorous, shell-pink Edwardian rose 'Souvenir de Saint Anne's',
in memory of a gentle wasp-waisted garden enthusiast of long ago.

*Plan of Butterstream*

1. Kitchen Garden
2. Stream
3. Gothic Bridge
4. Green Walk
5. Hot Coloured Garden
6. Tower & Blue Garden
7. White Garden
8. Herbaceous Borders
9. Laburnum Tunnel
10. Obelisk Garden
11. Italian Garden
12. Lawn & Summer House
13. Pavilions
14. Lime Allées & Canals

# CREAGH

## COUNTY CORK

Creagh's garden has been planted on the edge of the water, where the river runs into the sea between the towns of Baltimore and Skibbereen on the coast of West Cork. From the house you can see the small and verdant island of Inisbeg. It is a wild and romantic garden with two sides of the plantings hemmed in by sea wall and shore.

The garden is the life's work of a passionate gardener, the late Peter Harold-Barry. In 1937 Peter, from Ballyvonaire outside Buttevant in County Cork, married Gwendoline, the daughter of Sir Edmund Browne and his French wife. They had originally met as children in Youghal and were re-acquainted in England, where they were to marry in Westminster Cathedral. After the war in 1945, they bought Creagh as their family home. It was a happy, comfortable home, filled with interesting guests. In the winters, Peter and Gwen would retire to their house in Dublin, where they had many friends, among whom were writers such as Mary

*Previous page, main picture: A mossy tanglewood of beech and wild bluebells.*

*Previous page, detail: Raindrops on a flat yellow umbel of fennel.*

*Above: The view looking back towards the garden from the pebbled beach of the seashore with the tall Monterey pines of Sir John's Walk clearly visible and the distant church nearly hidden by trees.*

*Opposite: Sir John's Walk – an avenue of Monterey pines which can thrive even on the windswept coast. Monterey pine is now very rare in the wild, but is one of the most useful trees for sheltering seaside gardens.*

Lavin, and the famous genealogist and broadcaster, Pope O'Mahony. In 1963, however, their peaceful lives were shattered by the death in a car accident of their only daughter Christina. From this time, Gwen became a recluse until she died, while Peter, though still remaining cheerful, devoted himself ever more to the garden. Until a few months before his death in 1994, he was still planting new plants and looking at others as old friends. Peter had already begun opening the gardens to the public, and used to leave a bucket in the front porch as an honesty box into which visitors put their entrance money.

With the shoreline washed by the waves of the Gulf Stream, the growth in the garden is almost tropical. Peter's inspiration for the garden came from the paintings of the nineteenth-century French primitive painter Henri Rousseau, known as Le Douanier, and the plant picture that he succeeded in creating is exactly the sort of exotic environment in which it would not come as too great a surprise to see one of Rousseau's tigers glaring out from the prickly fronds. Essentially it is a wild garden in which plants have been allowed to become naturalized. They are not held in check except to ensure that they do not overwhelm their neighbours, which is the essence of the wild garden promoted by William Robinson. At Creagh, the mild and moist climate means that, as long as shelter is provided against storms and gales, subtropical species will thrive, and it can accommodate really exotic plants.

Peter's beloved tender fuchsias were planted against the dry stone walls of the grass-covered terrace that he built at the back of the house. This overlooks the sweep of the lawn ringed by trees and shrubs, on which fêtes, plays and charity open days are staged during the summer. A stone-flagged bridge leads into a wood with giant Chilean rhubarb and huge-leaved rhododendrons to left and right. Moving deeper into the wood, you pass azaleas, camellias and more rhododendrons. Yet further on, around a corner, in spring there is a superb carpet of bluebells, which are sheltered behind a hedge under the Scots pines. Ferns push up through the moss, and camellias are mixed with holly and escallonia. A field of Friesian cows completes the pastoral scene. Along the Fern Walk, past the donkeys in Malachy's Field, you finally reach the Boat House with its seaweed-covered slip built from slices of slate and sheltered by a fringe of wind-torn hazel. The triangle of meeting waters formed by the deep river constantly flowing into the tidal seabed can be seen from different angles through the cuts in the sea wall. Here, the Harold-Barrys used to board their launch to do the shopping in nearby Skibbereen, and the moss-covered deformed branches of an ancient beech still form a comfortable seat.

A small iron gate leads out of the wood and along the springy turf of Sir John's Walk, named after Sir John Wrixon-Becher, a former owner of the garden. The whistling wind can be heard in the treetops of the double avenue of huge Monterey pines (*Pinus radiata*) parallel to the shore. You emerge into the prettiest and most delicate woodland dotted with pale pink rhododendrons, flame-coloured Chilean fire-bushes (*Embothrium coccineum*) and *Magnolia x soulangeana*, its delicate white flowers flushed with pink. From a tunnel of laurel trees, you sometimes catch a glimpse of the water,

*Above: The neatly constructed hen house made from logs was influenced by the style of a Czechoslovakian mountain hut and put up in the walled garden in 1992.*

*Right: Salad greens and herbs with leeks, clipped box and a background of fennel in the walled vegetable garden.*

but otherwise you walk completely covered by the trees until you reach the grassy Quay. Here, there are benches on which you can sit and view at your leisure the little islands and the causeways along the Baltimore coast.

Originally, the present 20 acres of garden was a farm belonging to Fiernan O'Driscoll, until a family called Becher acquired the property of Creagh. The family at one time owned most of this part of West Cork, including Cape Clear, Sherkin and Mount Gabriel. The daughter of the house, Mary Becher, became the heiress because of a tragic accident in which her father shot her brother by mistake on his twenty-first birthday. Mary went on to marry into the Wrixons of Ballygiblin, who were a prominent Cork family famous for their hunting exploits. The Wrixon-Bechers, as they then became known, started building the Regency house, with its wide eaves and deep semi-circular bow: it was possibly intended to be a hunting lodge.

In 1819, their son William Wrixon-Becher MP married the famous Irish actress, the classical beauty Eliza O'Neil, in the church at Kilfane, County Kilkenny. It was Eliza who designed the serpentine pond and built the Gothic octagonal Folly between the pond and the sea. This now-ruined building is soon to be restored. From what you can make out, it must have had a downstairs room with a fireplace, perhaps in which to take tea and shelter from a squall, and then a staircase leads to the roof, where, on a clear day, there is a splendid watchtower's view of the estuary.

The pond next to the Folly is edged with green ferns, skunk cabbages (*Lysichiton americanus*), New Zealand flax (*Phormium tenax*) and Tasmanian tree ferns (*Dicksonia antarctica*), as well as more giant Chilean rhubarb, irises, primroses, weeping willows and bluebells. The moss-covered bark of sycamore and oaks is covered with ferns, and clumps of arum lilies (*Zantedeschia aethiopica*) have their roots deep in the pond bed, so that they appear to be growing on the water. The soil is acidic, which suits the late-summer hydrangea with its electric-blue flowers, and in the spring camellias abound.

Walking back up to the house, you pass a giant *Magnolia campbellii*, and suddenly a fragrant waft of vanilla warns you that you are approaching the *Azara microphylla* 'Variegata', which originated in William Gumbleton's magnificent garden at Belgrove, near Cobh, in the nineteenth century. On the lawn to the left of the front of the house is a thatched summerhouse, in which the Harold-Barrys used to play bridge. Peter called it his Baluba Folly, named after the fierce Baluba tribe in the Congo. He felt that it increased the Rousseau-like 'clearing in the jungle' impression. Next to the summerhouse is an Australian shrub not often seen in Irish gardens, the Braidwood waratah (*Telopea mongaensis*), which has bright red flowers in late spring.

Through camellia and pittosporum glades, and passing the *Rhododendron* 'Tally Ho', you come to the walled organic Kitchen Garden, which is currently undergoing restoration. Here are three series of restored glasshouses for ornamental and propagation purposes. The ornamental one has a flourishing lemon tree, with its delicious scent, and angels' trumpets (*Datura brugmansia aurea*), flowering quince and *Acacia longifolia*, Cape leadwort

*Top: After wintering in the greenhouse, the yellow flower of the aptly named angel's trumpet comes out in midsummer.*

*Above: Midsummer is also the time that these decorative ornamental gourds appear in the walled garden.*

*Above: The peat-stained water of the pond acts like a mirror, reflecting the interlaced branches of the trees.*

(*Plumbago auriculata*), jasmine and a banana passion-fruit (*Passiflora mollissima*), which actually produces tasty yellow banana-like fruits. A belt of tall beech trees shelters the garden from the elements.

A Czechoslovakian-style log hen house houses a variety of exotic fowl, such as Silkies, Morans, Plymouth Rocks, Bronze Turkeys and Guinea fowl, all of which scratch around making dust beds in what was the old orchard. Sorrel, leeks, broad beans, sprouting broccoli, globe artichokes, rhubarb, chives, mint and borage grow in boxwood-edged beds. There are edgings of wild strawberries and rows of raspberries. A cottage garden area at one end has clematis scrambling over wooden arches and a variety of flowering herbaceous plants with lots of different herbs, as well as comfrey. The comfrey is put in a large barrel and covered with water for six weeks, by which time it has turned into the most potent liquid manure.

In spring, the avenue in front of the house is filled with the scarlet flowers of the towering Chilean fire-bush next to tree-sized rhododendrons. Indian mallows (*Abutilon*), tree peonies, mimosa, which flowers in midwinter, and lots of magnolias flourish in the mild climate. The grass verges are left to grow wild with flowers such as bluebells, buttercups, scabious, cowslips and orchids. A south-facing herbaceous border against a thick yew hedge has been planted to screen off the car park. There is much wildlife in the gardens. Herons frequently examine the pond for delicacies and there are pheasants and partridges, barn owls and the little ring-necked doves that pair off for life.

Two friends of Peter Harold-Barry, Kenneth Lambert and Martin Sherry, who cared for him during his last years, have now lived here since 1991. Martin Sherry had previously worked for the National Trust in England and Kenneth Lambert is a conservator of houses and gardens. The work they undertook was tremendous, not only in the grounds, but also in the house itself. The garden had become very overgrown in the last years of Peter's life and they spent the first three years clearing and tidying, discovering lost vistas, making good the network of meandering paths, bringing in new top soil and cutting back the bamboo. Their determination and efforts have been helped by a team of gardeners from the Great Gardens of Ireland Restoration Programme. FAS, the state employment scheme, has also helped them. Their goal is to save as much of Peter Harold-Barry's beautiful garden and as many of his plants as possible. Their efforts in retaining the atmosphere of this balmy and aromatic place will surely encourage the summer visitors who flock to the sailing centre of nearby Baltimore to turn their rope-soled shoes towards exploring such a gentlemanly jungle.

*Above: The lush planting around the pond which Peter Harold-Barry devised in imitation of a jungle painted by the French artist Douanier Rousseau. The house seems to stand in a sunlit clearing.*

*Plan of Creagh*

1. Wood
2. Fern Walk
3. Malachy's Field
4. Boat House and Slip
5. Sir John's Walk
6. Quay
7. The Cache
8. Mill Pond
9. Old Mill Folly
10. Hen Hilton House
11. Kitchen Garden
12. Baluba Hut
13. Jungle Walk
14. Garden Entrance

# DERREEN

## COUNTY KERRY

Derreen stands as testimony to the extreme determination and foresight of one man, the fifth Marquis of Lansdowne (1845–1927), who inherited the demesne as a very young man in 1866. The gardens lie on a bare rocky promontory in the Bay of Kilmakilloge in the Barony of Glanerought, near Kenmare in County Kerry. Protected from the worst of the elements by the mountain of Knockatee at their rear and, on the other side of the bay, by a majestic-looking range of barren hills that stretches down the Beara Peninsula, it is amazing that these gardens were ever planted at all, given that their rocky wilderness location offered little top soil or shelter. The fourth Marquis of Lansdowne had initiated the planting of the area in 1863, but it was the fifth Marquis who really became fascinated by Derreen and began planting in 1870. He understood the potential of the soft Kerry climate, which suffers few frosts and has 2m (80in) of rainfall a year.

*Previous page, main picture: Antique rhododendrons drop scarlet petals on soft peaty soil – a scene repeated throughout the mild southwest of Ireland.*

*Previous page, detail: Where rhododendrons flourish, camellias will also thrive.*

*Above: A pirate's dream hideaway island, now linked to the mainland by a rickety bridge and so part of the garden.*

In addition, the fifth Marquis took advantage of the amazing array of plants and seeds that this country's intrepid explorers and professional plant-hunters were bringing to Ireland from all over the world. It was as if the deep mountain gorges of China, the rain forests of South America, the uplands of New Zealand and the native pine trees of British Columbia were all tipped into this pocket of profuse growth in an otherwise bare landscape in the west of Ireland. Dr Augustine Henry from County Londonderry had opened the treasure chest of China's wild flora while he served there as a customs official.

The 5th Marquis used to stay at Derreen with his wife for three months of every year from 1870 to the 1920s, except during the period between 1883 and 1894, when he was only able to snatch a few weeks between his postings, first to Canada as Governor General and then to India as Viceroy. Over the years, the gardens took shape, following his carefully laid-out plans.

The original scrub of hollies and brambles which covered the land was replaced with European black pines (*Pinus nigra*) and Monterey pines (*P. radiata*), as well as groups of griselinia, which are now 10m (35ft) high. Along the shoreline a belt of holm oak (*Quercus ilex*) and groups of the New Zealand flax (*Phormium tenax*), interspersed with *Olearia albida* and *Pittosporum tenuifolium*, were planted to shelter the rest of the gardens from the sea. Then the top soil was brought in. The huge drainage system, which criss-crosses the garden, was installed, providing essential drainage for the many rhododendron plants that were introduced in 1875. The fifth Marquis planted 100 *Rhododendron arboreum* hybrids, but before long they had grown to such a size that they were cutting off all light and air from the narrow walks. The decision was soon taken to cut most of them down. Today just a few specimens remain – all well over 18m (60ft). In the 1890s, the paths were

*Above: The placid waters and rugged mountains of Kilmakilloge Harbour. To create a garden here the first essential is shelter, so the pine trees were planted to provide this.*

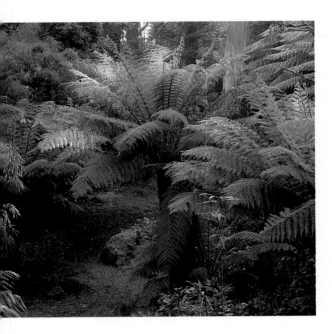

*Above: Tree ferns were once imported from New Zealand and Australia into Europe as ships' ballast. However, gardeners soon discovered that they would flourish in sheltered frost-free places. Now they are the quintessence of gardens in Cork and Kerry.*

*Opposite above: The young fronds of the tree ferns unfurl themselves from perfect fiddle heads. These specimens are probably more than a century old.*

*Opposite below: A majestic tree fern with its crown of feathery fronds is reaching sinuously towards the light from the dappled shade of the forest floor.*

laid out, the lawns were seeded and the sessile oaks (*Quercus petraea*) were cleared from around the house. Scots pines (*Pinus sylvestris*), groves of bamboo, tree ferns and shrubs of all kinds sheltered the lawns. The peat bank from which Lord Lansdowne's tenant would draw his household turf had been made into a bog garden, and the existence of the former farmland was only visible in places under the vegetation by the traces of a bank or ditch.

The house itself is swathed in gorgeous creepers. From the lawn, directly in front of the house, a smooth mound of rock emerges like a piece of moonstone left behind from the Ice Age. From here the vastness of the mountainous amphitheatre in which you are standing becomes apparent. Sheltered by the mountains and dark green conifers are three rhododendrons, two with delicate lemon flowers with a brown centre and one with pale pink flowers. In early spring, a carpet of bluebells surrounds an old Monterey pine. A Persian ironwood tree and an Irish yew frame this stunning Himalayan vista. From here to the Boat-house, you walk through a forest of rhododendrons and azaleas. In spring the path is flanked by a veritable array of colour, with pink, red and blue azaleas and a group of *Rhododendron* 'Fragrantissimum', whose white blossoms tinged with pink release a spicy nutmeg scent. A tall *Pieris formosa*, with lily-of-the-valley-shaped white flowers, stands next to a tree fern (*Dicksonia antarctica*). A *Rhododendron sinogrande* is protected by a staggeringly large *Chamaecyparis lawsonia* 'Erecta Viridis'.

Leaving the huge-leaved rhododendrons behind, you can cross a shaky wooden bridge to arrive at a small island packed with more pine and oak trees. As the tide goes out, the branches of oak trees hang with seaweed. During the eighteenth century, it is said that there was a souterrain on the island used to hide contraband, such as tobacco and brandy, which were smuggled into the bay by French ships. At this time, it seemed that everyone in the area was involved in smuggling, including the tenant of Derreen. 'Wool went out and brandy came in; everyone had a share of the profits and all were leagued together to defeat the officials of the government,' wrote the nineteenth-century historian J.A.Froude, who often stayed at Derreen and documented much of the local folklore in his book *The Two Chiefs of Dunboy*.

This treacherous part of the coast has seen many wrecks in its history. In his book *Glanerought and the Petty-Fitzmaurices* the sixth Marquis of Lansdowne recounts many stories, among them the fate of a West Indian merchantman, *The Planter*. In 1775, this ship, laden with silver and tea, reached Ballinaskelligs Bay in great distress. Lord Shelburne's tenant of Derreen at the time was Morty O'Sullivan McFinin Duff, Chief of the O'Sullivan clan. One of his illegitimate sons offered his services to *The Planter* and with great skill brought the half-disabled ship into Kilmackilloge harbour, conveniently close to his father's residence. The ship was promptly ransacked and became a total wreck. In those days, Morty O'Sullivan, with two near relations, controlled the whole of the western end of Glanerought, into which the representatives of the landlord seldom ventured with impunity. Once when Morty was an old sick man, Lord Shelburne sent a present of a case of claret. It is said that Morty dragged himself from his bed onto the big rock in front of the house and, with the most dreadful imprecations against the donor, solemnly broke every bottle – anything except undiluted spirits would have been considered an insult by the old chiefs of the clan O'Sullivan.

Looking back towards the house from the island, you can see nothing but a border of trees with the hills beyond. The gardens stay enclosed in a secret world. Turning into the Middle Walk, there stands the tree of *Rhododendron griffithianum* with its ethereal white flowers lighting up the dark shadows, and another rhododendron with blood-red trumpets. The grove of bamboo and forest of tree ferns are ringed by giant thujas, all of which combine to evoke a scene from a typical Japanese painting: a jungle seen through a gap in the trees, slate-grey sea, pine trees, wooden bridge and conical-shaped islands.

If you turn left again and take the granite steps up the hill, you enter a green tunnel and arrive into the light at Froude's Seat under the *Rhododendron* 'Loderi King George'. From here you can look out over the silvery water to the distant hills across the mussel beds. Here, in springtime, a grass path snakes through a mass of bluebells, which can be seen from the house. Conifers are interspersed with slender eucalyptus trees so tall you can't

*Above: The climate at Derreen being moist and mellow allows moss to cloak not just the tree trunks but also the outcrops of old red sandstone. When trees are toppled in storms they can still live on like this ancient* Cryptomeria japonica *'Elegans'.*

lean back far enough to see their tops. The tall evergreen Tasmanian Huon pine (*Lagarostrobus franklinii*) and Sawara cypress (*Chamaecyparis pisifera* 'Squarrosa') make you shiver in their shade. There are high banks of rock above the tree ferns, and rhododendrons light up the gloom in pale pink, true pink and purple. The granite hill has plants and trees growing along its banks as far as the sea, which arch up to reach the light. Walls of rock are covered in creepers like in a Brazilian jungle.

Turn left again into the King's Oozy, where King Edward VII and Queen Alexandra planted two commemorative bamboos in 1903. The area is made up of layer upon layer of leaf mould, and avenues of enormous tree ferns have seeded themselves with their roots in the drainage canals. A fragile young camellia flourishes in the shade of the rustling royal bamboos and the canopy of overhanging trees is now so high that it lets in enough light for plants to thrive below. *Rhododendron sinogrande*, *R. delavayi*, *R. falconeri* and *R. niveum* are now enormously tall, but the long vistas of clipped Victorian 'laurel lawns' that once surrounded them have long since gone.

Take the broad stone steps up from the King's Oozy and pass the biggest known specimen of *Cryptomeria japonica* 'Elegans'. Although its vertical height would reach 18m (60ft), since being damaged by a gale it has been supported horizontally 2m (6ft) above its original position on what is known as the Glade Walk. Every tree trunk is deep in moss; the rocks too are smothered in moss and liverworts. Moving on, you might breathe a sigh of relief once you have passed the menacing-looking Patagonian cypresses (*Fitzroya cupressoides*) with their overhanging branches and reached a little terrace cut into the cliff-face. Here, at dusk, you can sit on the Knockatee Seat and watch the granite face of that mountain slowly turning pink as the sun sets. Directly below, the chasm is filled with a single rhododendron, which is covered in masses of rose-coloured flowers in spring.

It is said that the fifth Marquis employed 40 people to create the garden. While in India, he was ideally positioned to bring back rare species from the East, subscribing to the Himalayan plant-hunting expeditions. He also bought many exotic plants from the famous nursery firm of Veitch, and also from the Waterer nurseries at Sunningdale in Berkshire, England. In the true tradition of William Robinson, the naturalization of hardy and exotic plants from other countries was such a success that these original plants have spread into large groups of tree ferns, myrtles and several species of *Gaultheria*. The Chilean lantern trees (*Crinodendron hookerianum*) and fire-bushes (*Embothrium coccineum*) do as well here as in their native habitat, as do the tall acacias from Australia. The *Eucalyptus globulus* were planted at Derreen as early as 1870 and are among the largest recorded in cultivation. *Drimys winteri*, *Clethra alnifolia*, *Myrtus luma* and *M. lechleriana*, as well as the tree ferns (*Dicksonia antarctica*) all flourish in this warm climate and mountain setting.

Like Creagh, this is another Robinsonian garden, with the advantage that the planting is older and covers a larger area. The tree ferns are naturalized and the bamboo rampant, and, although a period of neglect allowed them to run wild, they have been hacked back and the skeletons of mature trees resuscitated. There is a published record of the early planting in the form of a catalogue, and, in some ways, Derreen was a trial ground (like the nearby garden of Rossdohan) for plants from Australia and New Zealand. The astonishingly fast rate of growth of many of the species meant that the fifth Marquis was able to see his treasures mature in his own lifetime.

After a long period of inactivity, the estate was inherited by Viscountess Mersey, the granddaughter of the fifth Marquis. She was a keen gardener, who breathed new life into the gardens. Derreen is now owned by her son and daughter-in-law, Mr and Mrs David Bigham, who love the garden with a passion. They have recently opened the gates to the public.

*Plan of Derreen Gardens*

1. Rock
2. Broad Walk
3. New Ponds
4. Boat House Walk
5. Froude's Seat
6. Middle Walk
7. Boat House
8. Island
9. Ladies Bathing Place
10. King's Oozy
11. Kilmakilloge Harbour
12. Little Oozy
13. Knockatee Seat
14. Goleen Walk

# THE DILLON GARDEN
## RANELAGH, DUBLIN

Helen Dillon's walled town garden is in the centre of Dublin and yet tucked away off a main thoroughfare down a shaded cul-de-sac. The entrance to her secret world is a simple wooden gate. On the day of my visit, there had just been a rain shower and shafts of sunlight were streaming onto the front steps of the plain, square Georgian villa. The door was thrown open by a beaming figure with short blonde hair and cornflower-blue eyes who wailed in despair, 'I can't think why you have come today – there is nothing to see in the garden at all!' Helen Dillon's anxiety has not lessened as she has become famous; in fact, as the reviews of her books, her journalism, her lectures, her television appearances and her garden become increasingly flattering, her artist's desire for perfection, unachievable in her own eyes, reaches agonizing proportions. Twenty-six years ago Helen and her husband Val walked through the door of 45 Sandford Road and fell in love with the house and what was then

*Previous page, main picture: William Robinson said that the Californian tree poppy (Romneya coulteri) was 'the fairest plant that ever came to our land from that country of flowers'. It is wilful but very beautiful.*

*Previous page, detail: Blue delphiniums are just one of the many attractions in the Dillon garden.*

*Above: The informal pavement in the front garden is a foil for foliage and flowers. The large terracotta jar is planted with a trailing raspberry.*

an ordinary Dublin walled town garden. They have been working on it ever since they moved in, and when they are not toiling in the garden, they can sit in their butter-yellow drawing room and look out through its long windows at the garden, with its emerald-green lawn and thickly planted borders. It seemed a good omen that Dr Augustine Henry, the Edwardian plant collector, had lived next door, and that his light orange, faintly spotted *Lilium henryi*, which he brought back from the limestone hills of China, was flourishing at over 2m (7ft).

Brought up in the highlands of Scotland, Helen has been a gardener ever since a geranium was given to her when she was just a child. She is a voracious plant collector and Ireland's temperate climate means that she is spoilt for choice in the range of plants she can cultivate. Each year she travels abroad far and wide, bringing back treasures of seeds from the Himalayas, the Alps, New Zealand, South Africa and South and North America, and propagating them all in her greenhouse. The result is a plantsman's garden containing hundreds of plants on just under one acre of land. Seemingly effortlessly, she brings all the plants together to create a garden that is both attractive and well balanced. Each plant is given the right soil and other growing conditions that would most resemble its natural habitat. She has a crusading desire to encourage American gardeners to try out new plants, and her book *Garden Artistry* is written with special reference to American zones of climate related to the plants that she can grow in Ireland which she thinks would flourish there as well.

Helen also has a burning passion for old cultivars. She spends any spare time searching derelict gardens for old-fashioned plants that need rescuing from obscurity or oblivion, such as the garden forms of wild plants like the double buttercup, the hen-and-chickens daisy and the crested ferns. Some of the plants that were grown at the beginning of the century that have died out in mainland Europe and England are still flourishing in her garden. The English National Trust's plant cataloguer was astonished to find the long-vanished old double red nasturtium still doing well in Ireland. Helen thinks that this is because the landscape and gardens of Ireland have not suffered the same changes of use as those in other parts of Europe, in addition to being unaffected by the damage caused by two world wars. She is particularly attached to plants with Irish connections and *Viola* 'Irish Molly', *Agapanthus* 'Lady Moore' and *Celmisia* 'David Shackleton' (named after her mentor who built up his famous plant collection in another walled garden at Beech Park, County Dublin) have pride of place. Some of her plants have come in direct line from long-departed gardeners of their day and she feels she has been lucky to have known the tail-end of the last of the old Irish gardeners. Some of the gardeners she met for lunch would give gems of plants, with the entreaty that she didn't give them away. Helen's attitude is different and she wants to encourage the world to grow these plants.

Nothing has been more influential in encouraging the rising tide of interest in Irish gardens than the publication of Helen's first book, *In an*

*Irish Garden*, which she wrote with the famous designer the late Sybil Connolly. Her latest book, entitled *Helen Dillon on Gardening*, is a compilation of her weekly gardening columns which feature in the *Sunday Tribune*: these are as encouraging and instructive as anything by Vita Sackville-West or Anne Scott-James.

To use a garden as a canvas for aesthetic effect requires a deep knowledge and love of plants, along with the courage and energy to be prepared to uproot and move existing plants to create the desired overall design. 'My fingers are worn to the bone,' Helen sighs, 'but the garden is never right.' She and Val do by far the majority of the work in the garden themselves, prompting sympathetic Americans to send them special soothing hand creams on occasion! A robin, in what must now have become a hereditary position, either sits on Val's shoulder or near at hand. Helen's nickname for Val is Grub, and he lives upto his name by taking care of the compost heap. Housed in the brick courtyard at the side of the house where the carriages would have been kept, comes the delicious smell of freshly mown grass. All the garden material, including dead flowers, is shredded and forked into bays with wooden slatted moveable fronts, where it gradually decomposes and rots down into beautiful friable compost.

*Below: The dominant colours in early summer are magentas and purples. The tall grass is a fountain of gold while the modern English rose 'Graham Stuart Thomas' contributes a splash of yellow. Standard wisteria, lots of cranesbill, spiky foliage of red hot pokers and irises, alliums, as well as alpine beds in the gravel form the structure of the front garden.*

Walking down the steps from the house with the wide green lawn edged by clipped pyramids of box stretching ahead of you, two ivy-trimmed stone sphinxes guard the south-facing terrace. Broad, thickly planted borders on either side of the lawn, inspired by the colour combinations at Mount Stewart, County Down, are themselves dissected by almost invisible narrow stone paths. You feel as though you are standing in the middle of the border itself.

Helen's borders are so memorable because she has succeeded in creating a 'heavenly muddle'. Angel's fishing rods (*Dierama pulcherrimum*) brush your arms as you pass, admiring the cloudy blues and airy mauves in the right-hand border, and hot velvety reds paling to pinks in the left. Everything is flourishing so finely and there are so many faces of flowers, some hanging in bells and some in bunches, that it is hard to believe that so many plants

*Above: Here Helen has arranged pots of choice alpines to provide continual colour and interest; they can be protected in the winter. They are arranged on antique cast iron tables.*

in such a complex plan could be fitted into what is such a deceptively simple-looking structure. However, she explains that some plants just can't stand the pace, and get squashed to death.

At the end of the green lawn there is a round pond, formal in style, with a fountain, and an Arbour in the centre of a series of arches which is draped with climbers. There are apple trees, a Judas tree and clipped juniper, while roses and honeysuckle tumble over the arches with foxgloves sheltering underneath them. If you turn right off the lawn and pass between two little sturdy box pillars, you will find the greenhouse which is always bursting with delicate, scented, half-hardy plants.

A series of garden compartments leads you around the edge of the garden walls. The south wall of the house is covered with climbers, including the sage

*Above: Variegated foliage of euonymus and ceanothus provides year-round cream and gold while the perennials come and go.*

*Opposite: Helen takes every opportunity to use clipped box in the Yellow Garden. Two dwarf cones of box are almost smothered by a mélange of yellow and orange flowers and green and silver foliage in her recently planted yellow border.*

greens and the powdery greys of the leaves of *Vitis vinifera* 'Incana' with its edible black grapes. *Bomaria caldesii* is related to an alstroemeria, and the flowers of the *Ixia viridiflora* from South Africa look like turquoise-coloured tissue paper. A plant that Helen tells us we will not often find in the U. K. is *Billardiera longiflora* from Tasmania, which has shiny navy blue berries and pale yellow flowers. There are pansies, and an *Abutilon megapotamicum* with its red petticoat petals. Pots adorn the terrace and pans of alpines stand on the wrought-iron tables. The white and pink daisy-like stars of *Rhodohypoxis* come from the Drakensburg mountains in South Africa and will flower for three months as long as you water them all throughout the summer and keep them dry in the winter (to remind them of being covered by snow) in their terracotta alpine pans.

Walking round the garden it becomes evident that the story of its development reflects the story of Helen's life. Many of the plants in the garden hold precious memories for her, and she refers to them as fondly as she would to special friends or relatives, adding to the intimate atmosphere of this intensely personal garden. She proudly introduces me to the 'Duchesse de Brabant', a pale apricot tea rose that she was given as a cutting in a graveyard in Virginia – it is the rose that Teddy Roosevelt always wore in his buttonhole. A bearded light blue iris, which is an old cultivar, was given to her by the great horticulturist Graham Stuart Thomas, and a cousin brought her back the rose 'Marie Pavie' that is climbing on the trellis from his holidays. We gaze down at what appears to be a piece of mauve ruched taffeta striped in pink, which she tells me is an old Irish rose that she came across in a forgotten garden in County Westmeath. In passing, she remarks that the little fat bells of *Clematis* 'Crispa' look like old fashioned bonnets.

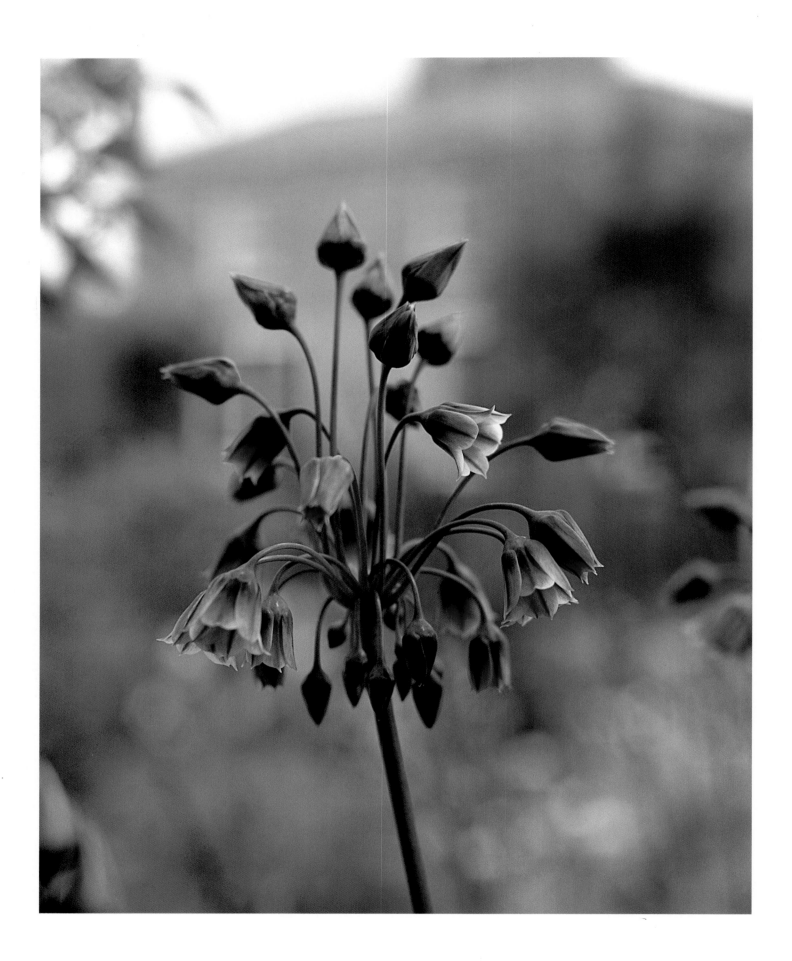

She next introduces the only American resident in the garden, *Clematis viticella*, 'Mrs Betty Corning', and I feel as though I am meeting the very lady herself. She admits that the *Michauxia* seed which she brought back from Syria was very easy to grow – it now looks like an enormous, upside-down passionflower. The *Nectaroscordum siculum* she describes as coming out in 'umbrella-mode', with its little harebell-like, dusty pink flower heads sticking out on long thin stalks. The metre-high (3ft) *Clematis integrifolia* is admirably displayed in a smart metal basket, an idea for a plant support that she got from Mrs Betty Farquar, who in turn copied it from the Duchess of Devonshire. *Allium cristophii* has thousands of mauve stars forming a big ball. Alongside these plants is the rather phallic *Puya alpestris*, whose fat buds, as Helen explains with a chortle, elongate and then erupt into iridescent, shiny green bells.

There are dense mounds in the gravel of the most unusual alpines and different-coloured starry flower heads look up out of the stone troughs.

Alpines greet you as well when you enter into the front garden, which has recently undergone a transformation from being a mass of plants that were difficult to see properly into a much more open and easily accessible space. A paved terrace of silvery grey Donegal flags is now surrounded by judiciously chosen, carefully placed plants so that it is pure delight to sit on the stone seat in the calm of the evening sunshine by colour and scent.

One of Helen's worries about her garden is that people will feel intimidated by seeing so many plants in such a comparatively small space. It most certainly is a specialist's garden in many ways, but that does not stop the rest of us from enjoying the wonders it has to offer. She is doing her best to de-mystify gardening. 'I want my garden' she says simply, 'to make people feel better.'

*Opposite: Graham Stuart Thomas, the doyen of English gardeners and one of Helen's 'mentors', advises that this elegant onion can become a nuisance!* Nectaroscordum siculum *comes from the Balkans and its seed heads are as elegant as its bell-shaped flowers on their long thin stalks. The flowers hang down before they are fertilized and then stand up again like small umbrellas.*

*Below left: The rare old* Begonia *'Hatton Castle' on two terracotta pots at the edge of the path that winds behind the Red Border, which is at its best in July.*

*Below right: Two reds that complement each other in the Red Border are the darkest red* Scabiosa *'Chile Black' next to the startling lobelias.*

# GLENVEAGH CASTLE
## COUNTY DONEGAL

Glenveagh Castle is a battlemented, cut-stone, Victorian hunting lodge with a tower and a courtyard built overlooking the blue waters of Lough Veagh. It is surrounded by almost tropically luxuriant gardens in the middle of a valley that was formed during several ice ages. The snout of a glacier ground its way through the encircling sheer granite mountains, leaving behind lakes and streams, corries and glens, which now form the wild and savage scenery of a 25,000 acre National Park.

Before the Irish State took over the conservation of the gardens, there was a long-running American connection with Glenveagh. It began in 1861, when its archetypal wicked Irish landlord, John George Adair, married a beautiful, wealthy, young American widow called Cornelia Richie. Her sweetness and good sense had prevailed over the local people's bitter dislike of her husband, who had been responsible for evicting 46 of his tenants' families during and after the Famine.

*Previous page, main picture: The turret of Glenveagh Castle seen through a tracery of mountain ash, a tree that is native in Ireland. The red berries are usually devoured rapidly by the birds.*

*Previous page, detail: Dahlia 'Matt Armour', a variety unique to Glenveagh, named after a former head gardener.*

*Above: Henry McIlhenny created this formal 'potager' at Glenveagh.*

After his death in 1885, Cornelia continued to live at Glenveagh until a few years before her own death in 1921. She introduced deer-stalking in the 1890s and, for the next 30 years, spent most of her time in County Donegal, entertaining streams of visitors, laying out the gardens, and planting and improving the rugged terrain around the castle. During the First World War, she allowed Glenveagh to be used as a convalescent home for wounded Belgian soldiers. After her death, it was occupied in quick succession by both sides in the Irish Civil War of 1922. A Harvard professor, Arthur Kingsley Porter, and his wife then bought it in 1929. Here he was to write his book *The Crosses and Culture of Ireland*, before disappearing in mysterious circumstances while on a walk on the island of Inishbofin.

In 1936 another American with links in the locality, Henry McIlhenny, bought the property. His grandfather had grown up near Glenveagh in the small village of Milford. After emigrating to Columbus, Georgia, he settled in Philadelphia, where he made a fortune from inventing the first gas meter. On the staff of the Philadelphia Museum of Art, and then, after his retirement, chairman of the Board of Trustees, Henry McIlhenny was a connoisseur and collector of paintings and furniture with which he filled the castle.

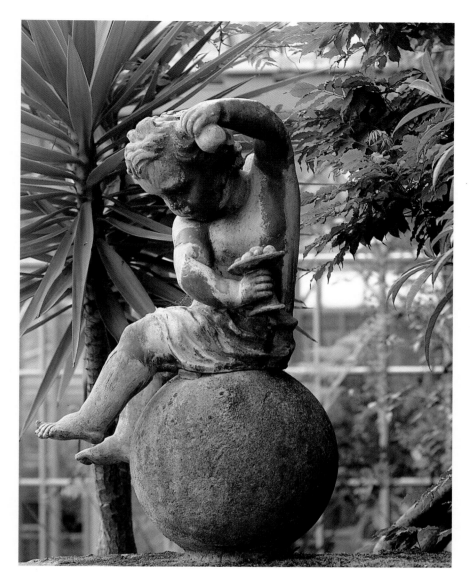

His hospitality and generosity at Glenveagh was legendary. Between 1947 and 1983, he must have entertained thousands of people in his highland retreat. He had friends all over the world, including members of the establishment and scholars, as well as numerous poets, painters, authors, musicians, actors, dancers and even movie stars. They enjoyed his company; he was an exceptionally genial host with an extraordinary store of amusing anecdotes and witty gossip. An invitation to Glenveagh was much sought after and discussed, and there was nothing he liked better during the 1950s, 60s and 70s than sending the car to the airport to collect the latest visitor, perhaps Grace Kelly or Greta Garbo, and to bring them to his romantic, lonely castle.

A knowledgeable gardener himself, Henry McIlhenny employed both Lanning Roper and Jim Russell to help with the gardens. They grew year after year for 46 years so that the hedges, flowerbeds, staircases, arches, walls, stone urns, stags, eagles, and pillars framing vistas became countless. Going on a tour of the garden with Henry McIlhenny, as Desmond Guinness remembers, was always rather like being introduced to various guests at a cocktail party. 'This plant was given to me by Lady Leitrim, and this very distinguished one here by Rear Admiral Stevenson', and so on.

*Above centre: The summer display of the Dahlia 'Matt Armour', which was raised at Glenveagh perhaps 50 years ago and has been a permanent fixture since in this varied and ornamental garden.*

*Above: This small lead cherub holding a pear in one hand, a fruit dish in the other and sitting on top of a stone ball outside the orangerie is just one of the many decorative figures in the Walled Garden.*

Garden leads into garden at Glenveagh with bemusing variety, each one hidden from the next, and each one either gazing inward and thickly surrounded by shelter, or else preparing you with a build-up of well-chosen trees and shrubs for a dramatic outward view of hillside and lake. Desmond Guinness recalls Henry saying: 'I just can't STAND earth', giving the offending substance a fierce prod with his stick and instructing his Head Gardener to see that it was covered with greenery. The vegetable plots in the Walled Garden were all edged with wild strawberries at his special request, and Philippe Jullian designed him an *orangerie* in which to grow exotics and to drink coffee after dinner on summer evenings.

Benevolent and well-organized in everything he did, Henry sold the estate in 1975 to the Irish Office of Public Works to create a National Park, now under the care of Dúchas, the Heritage Service of the Department of Arts, Gaeltacht, and the Islands, and in 1983 he gave the castle and gardens to the nation so that in 1986 the castle was opened to the public just a few months after he had died. It is a strange sensation arriving at the gardens today without its charismatic creator, but it is a compliment to his judgement and taste to see how the planting has matured, and that such a success has been made of the gardens by Dúchas. As is inevitable over a period of time, some details have changed, but the overall effect is splendid and one really expects Henry McIlhenny to appear beaming at the entrance to the courtyard around which he had added more battlements to increase the picturesque effect. I think he would be proud and happy if he could see how it all looks today.

Take the road that leads to the castle winding along the blue lake past mountains, yellow gorse and silver birches, until you arrive at the Eagle Gate and enter the avenue bordered by rhododendron hedges and banks of hydrangeas leading up to the castle. Here you can take tea in the sunny courtyard paved with black and grey marble, where terracotta lemon pots are planted with azaleas, figs and camellias. Lining the walls are bushes of bay, trimmed by the frothy leaves of lady's mantle (*Alchemilla mollis*).

The grey stone castle sits on the grass terrace above the lake. The grimness of cut stone is softened by banks of fuchsia clipped and trained to climb and spread up the walls. The weather here is extremely changeable. Wind is a major hazard, with gales raging through the glen. Calm water can quickly become a seething mass of waves and flying spume. The rainfall is high with roughly 1.8m (70in) a year and, due to the influence of the Gulf Stream,

*Above: The stark contrast between the wild and the cultivated. On the far side of Lough Veagh the rocks and the moorland are in their natural state, while on the near side, thickly planted pine trees shelter the castle and its gardens, creating an exceptional micro-climate.*

*Opposite above: Henry McIlhenny was a discerning collector of antique garden ornaments which are a feature of Glenveagh.*

*Opposite below: Great Aztec-like flights of steps leading to a viewing platform from which the photograph on this page was taken.*

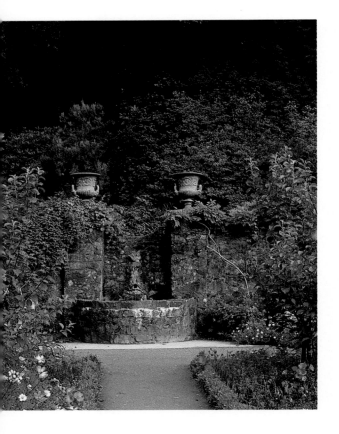

the winters are mild with little frost and only occasional snow. Windbreaks of Scots and Austrian pines, alders, *Rhododendron ponticum* (which has become a pest), escallonias, olearias and bamboo were all planted early on and provide invaluable shelter. The peaty soil is acidic and in places trees are hard to grow, but palms, tree ferns, mimosas, and fragrant rhododendrons, which usually live in a greenhouse, and a wide variety of tender plants can all flourish out of doors. Peat and farmyard manure are invaluable for improving the soil.

A path leads from a boathouse to the formal Italian Garden on the south side, where a rectangle of grass is enclosed by clipped griselinia hedges lined with busts of Roman emperors on ivy-clad piers, life-size stone sculptures and a large seat. It is a soothing green outdoor room, with few flowers, although tall rhododendrons, mostly blue *R. augustinii* and late-flowering white hybrids, shelter within the hedges. In summer, eucryphias make tall pillars of white against the green background. It is heartening to know that the seemingly frail eucryphias can stand up to the unpredictable gusting winds.

The Pleasure Ground, to the north of the castle, is a broad sweep of lawn that mimics the contours of the lake. It is completely enclosed by shrubs and trees planted on the edge of the surrounding mountain gorges among streams hidden by ferny fronds. The green tapestry is subtly highlighted by occasional batches of colour – the fiery leaves of a Japanese maple or the springtime blooms of primulas whose seed was collected from Yunnan. There are tree ferns and Chusan palms, and the autumn-colouring katsura tree (*Cercidiphyllum japonicum*). Several tall tree rhododendrons, including *R. falconeri* and *R. sinogrande*, with their very large leaves and pale yellow flowers, were transplanted from nearby Mulroy House in the 1950s. Hoherias, *Drimys winteri* and eucryphia reach up into the sheltering pines next to grimacing Balinese sculptures and bright green Japanese *Trochodendron aralioides* trees. Different coloured lichens splay along their branches. The snowdrop tree (*Styrax japonica*) has been cleverly planted hanging over the path, so that in the summer months you can look up to see a spangle of white flowers above you against the inky green of the tangled leaves and branches.

On the way to the Italian Terrace the classic Irish late-summer combination of montbretia, with its cheerful orange sprays and sharp bright green leaves, and hydrangea, with pale blue blossoms, lines the path. In the distance, through the pine trees, you can glimpse a column topped by a stone pineapple, the symbol of hospitality. Past the Himalayan Garden that is filled in spring with *Meconopsis nepalensis* and has a Ganesh seated tranquilly by the pond, and past the Belgian Walk, built by convalescing Belgians and shaded by a group of *Eucryphia moorei*, you reach the Italian Terrace which was designed by Lanning Roper in 1965 with statues and herms chosen by the owner. It is surrounded by rhododendrons and azaleas and has a *Metrosideros umbellata*, which is a mass of red spikes in midsummer. A marble seat offers the opportunity for a welcome rest, surrounded by the humming of bees.

After you have walked on a short way, the calm that has been distilled from these shady groves of plants and trees is suddenly shattered as you go through yet another exotic urn-topped gate into the riot of colour and activity in the French-style *jardin potager* inside the Walled Garden. Nothing is hidden from view and a swathe of old-fashioned red dahlias cuts across one end in front of the elegant Gothic Conservatory. Vegetables and fruit trees are planted in neat rows between hedges, with spirals of clipped boxwood at each end. There is a brick terrace and standard bay trees in pots. Apple trees, fruit bushes, sweet peas, roses, artichokes, beetroot, potatoes, runner beans, peas, borage and mint are all in beds divided down the middle by two great herbaceous borders. Each garden gate has a different feature on the top of the piers and water bubbles from a stone dolphin fountain built into the wall.

Slipping through a gate you come to a lovely rocky glen with moss-covered rocks and trees. Here there is a steeply rising flight of 67 steps – dramatic in their austere, almost Aztec simplicity – which, if not leading to a heart attack, certainly nowhere else, because at the top all that is waiting is the most incredibly beautiful view of the castle, lake and mountainside. In spring, the steps are surrounded by a huge mass of white flushed with pink, heavily scented *Rhododendron ciliatum*, which seeds freely in the moss.

Throughout the garden there are different views across the landscape, all carefully hidden by hedges and planted areas until the last minute. Finding a seat in a clearing from which you can enjoy a panorama of breath-taking natural beauty is one of the abiding joys of this garden.

*Above: A close-up of the fountain which shows the detail of the dolphins.*

*Opposite above: The ornamental dolphin fountain with vases is located in the potager.*

*Opposite below: Young apple trees under planted with pink mallows to provide colour in the upper section of the potager – in the distance are the white flowers of eucryphia.*

*Plan of Glenveagh Castle*

1. Boat House
2. Italian Garden
3. Swiss Walk
4. View Garden
5. Rose Garden
6. Walled Garden
7. 67 Steps
8. Viewing Terrace
9. Belgian Walk
10. Himalayan Garden
11. Italian Terrace
12. Pleasure Ground
13. Lough Veagh

# GLIN CASTLE
## COUNTY LIMERICK

The gardens at Glin Castle are in a continuous state of rediscovery and re-creation, and there is always something to learn about their history and horticulture. Precariously balanced on the banks of the River Shannon as it roars towards its tidal estuary, the castle itself stands braced to withstand the full onslaught of the Atlantic weather, thereby protecting the gardens that flow gently up the hill behind it. Viewed from a boat on the water, the castle presents a fairytale façade as it nestles among high trees between blue bands of water and sky. Its setting in the landscape is highly dramatic and the more I live here, the more I wonder at the subtlety and good sense of the original builders. A network of box-drains, lined and edged with stone, some at an extraordinary depth of 4m (13ft), criss-cross the garden, guiding turbulent springs away from the house and keeping the garden as dry as possible. In early February, the field that runs down to the river in front of the house is glassy with water from the rising high neap-tides.

*Previous page, main picture: Lupins, clipped box and golden Irish yews frame the rustic temple used to shelter from the gentle spring rain. It is made from wood thinnings and strategically placed rope, and is built into the stone wall as the focus for the path that divides the upper end of the walled garden.*

*Previous page, detail: The rose called 'Narrow Water' has never flowered better since its move from the Walled Garden to a new position by the edge of the stream in the Pleasure Grounds.*

*Above: A ring of mock standing stones situated high on a bank behind the Pleasure Grounds. From here there is a heady view between the trees to the River Shannon below.*

The first Norman FitzGerald castle in Limerick was Shanid, built in 1197, now a ruined fragment of a keep on a tall motte high above the pasture lands of West Limerick, about 13km (8 miles) from Glin. 'Shanid-Abu', meaning 'Shanid for ever', was the Geraldine war cry, which decorates the plaster ceilings in the present castle The first recorded entry for the Knight of Glin is in documents dated 1425. Here the Geraldines built a castle on the little river that runs into the Shannon, where they lived speaking Gaelic, marrying daughters of neighbouring chieftains and leading a feudal life. They owned many of the castles between Glin and Limerick and many thousands of acres of land. Finally, this castle in Glin was besieged and razed to the ground by Queen Elizabeth's general, Sir George Carew, in 1600, leaving only the stone stump with a gaping empty window that you see on driving into the village today. After this calamity the Geraldines lived in hiding in fear of their lives, until they moved to exactly the place where I live today. They built the long, low, thatched house one room thick, and this eventually evolved into the two-storied wing of the present Glin Castle.

Colonel John Batemen FitzGerald, the twenty-fourth Knight of Glin, began building the main part of the castle – a plain, bow-windowed Georgian house – about 1780. His English wife, Margaretta Maria Fraunceis Gwyn took particular interest in the delicate plasterwork of the hall, from harps and spidery vines to the garlands of flowers and sheaves of wheat that decorate the ceiling. There are plasterwork dolphins which reflect the real-life ones to be seen on the river, and over the Venetian window looking out over the garden

*Above: The remains of a Victorian garden with tree ferns and bamboos led up to this forgotten early nineteenth century Hermitage that was hidden in brambles. It now stands in a glade surrounded by young oak trees.*

from the flying staircase float white plasterwork cornucopias. There must have been a garden of sorts when the house was first built, but it appears that military matters were uppermost in the twenty-fourth Knight of Glin's thoughts. Their only son, John Fraunceis FitzGerald, was only 12 when his father died in 1803, and so returned to his grandparents' house to be brought up at Forde Abbey in Dorset, England, where there were extensive gardens.

On graduating from Cambridge, John Fraunceis returned to Glin, and was determined to embellish his demesne in a manner befitting his family's romantic past. He castellated the house and stableyard with pastrycook battlements, built gimcrack Gothic lodges at each gate, a tiny white castellated eye-catcher (the bathing lodge) on the edge of the river, the high stone-walled Kitchen Garden, and a Hermitage on the hill behind the Pleasure Grounds. He brought over a gardener, one William Bicknell from Somerset, in 1822 to lay out the plantations, and the bones of the garden were put in place. In place of the old road that cut through the demesne, he arranged for the engineer Alexander Nimmo to build a new road and sea wall. This imposing road, cleverly hidden from view by a splendid new ha-ha constructed to hold back the front field, now snaked along the coast. Travellers from Foynes to Tarbert now had a much easier journey, as they were saved the laborious climb up the muddy hill through the middle of the crusty knight's demesne. Today, peering out of the dining-room windows, you will sometimes see the oddly disconnected top of a passing school bus apparently floating unaided along the top of the ha-ha.

*Above: A formal garden room without walls tempts you out of the castle onto the terrace that is trimmed with huge balls and standard domes of clipped bay. The yellow Banksian rose clambers around the crenellations and all is sheltered by a Monterey pine.*

The entrance to the property now took the visitor through the new Gothic lodge in the village, in which the 'Knight of the Women' or '*ridire na mBan*' as John Fraunceis became known locally, installed his mistress. Entering a long avenue of trees, a thick band of woodland cut off all sight of the water until you rounded a corner. Emerging out of the green gloom into the light again, the impact of the view before you would have been, as it is now, breathtaking. A huge green field slopes down towards the wide, sparkling river with the white bathing lodge outlined against it, and the whole of County Clare seems to be laid out in front of you on the other side of the water. On a clear day, you can see the mountains, the Twelve Pins of Galway, in the misty distance.

Not much has changed since those days, except that great stands of Chilean rhubarb line the road before you reach this view, and Tom Wall, the gardener, has taken the place of the mistress in the lodge! After the Famine and during Victorian times, nothing very much happened and the family lived frugally with no extra cash to expand or change the buildings or the garden.

*Above: A blindingly white early nineteenth century 'eye-catcher' like a toy fort sits atop the ha-ha overlooking the River Shannon. For many years it was used as a bathing lodge.*

The 'Cracked Knight' (John Francis Eyre FitzGerald, son of the 'Knight of the Women') rode his horse up the front stairs, and his son the 'Big Knight' downed a bottle of whiskey a day while his sensible wife steered the estate safely through the Land Wars. Then, in 1892, the garden sprang to life again with the marriage of my husband's grandfather to Lady Rachel Wyndham Quin. Sensitive and artistic, she planted the hill behind the house with thousands of daffodil bulbs given to her by her friends the Dorrien Smiths of Tresco on the Isles of Scilly. She planted the specimen conifers, the Chilean lantern bush (*Crinodendron hookerianum*), the monumental red cedars (*Thuja plicata*), the *Drimys winteri* and the now massive *Pinus radiata* beside the castle. Had she lived longer, the garden would certainly have flourished. Yet, sadly, she was to die young, soon after my father-in-law's birth, and a cloak of sadness fell over the whole demesne. My husband's grandfather had a stroke in 1910 which left him in a wheelchair and life was pretty miserable until my mother-in-law, Veronica Milner, came here as a girl of 18 in 1929.

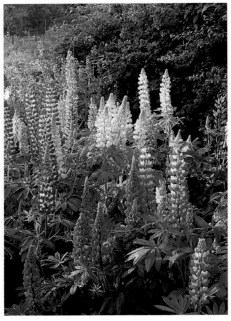

*Above: Pink and white cosmos mean mid-summer in the walled garden.*

*Above below: Lupins have always been grown at the foot of the greenhouse steps.*

*Right: An avenue of clipped yews in their steel corsets divide the walled garden and are seen through a fuchsia tunnel. The comfortable Edwardian garden seat beckons on hot sunny afternoons.*

Veronica immediately set about brightening up the whole place. Clearing away the laurels and brambles that were growing up to the windows and executing the pampas grass on the lawn, she re-cast the formal paths as we see them today and planted all the lovely magnolias, cherries and dogwoods that flutter and glimmer in spring along the sides of the lawns. The sprawling Himalayan dogwood is covered in white blossoms in spring and produces strawberry-like fruit in summer. The sundial in the middle of the lawn was surrounded by a yew hedge and she built the low, swooping wall that divides the garden from the daffodil hill, centring it with a graceful Persian ironwood tree (*Parrotia persica*). Veronica also planted the simple green rectangle of hedge with curving ends outside the drawing-room windows and planted snowdrops in circles around all the trees. In her day, the castle was white-washed every summer by two men suspended in baskets, swinging somewhat precariously from the battlements.

On the garden side of the castle, she laid down a terrace of Liscannor flags and planted two standard pom-poms of bay, which have now become two great bell-shaped domes. Her yellow Banksian rose twines around the smoking-room window. In spring, the ground around the oak tree on the hill is covered with bluebells. Pale-coloured rhododendrons line the path to the stream. Also in spring, the kowhai from New Zealand stands in a pool of saffron-coloured pollen across the path from the tall *Magnolia campbellii*, with its wine glass-shaped pink petals that are blown all over the lawn in March. Veronica took cuttings of the camellia trees at nearby Tarbert House which quickly grew into abundant shrubs bearing stiff, scarlet flowers with pointed petals, which have flowered profusely ever since. A side avenue of cordylines leads to a white embroidered wrought-iron gate in the garden wall.

During the Second World War, my mother-in-law sold the produce of the Kitchen Garden to the infant Shannon Airport at nearby Foynes. Sea-planes landed here with their glamorous passengers, including European kings and queens, diplomats, American generals, spies and even film stars. All the passengers needed to be fed and were often brought home to Glin to stay.

My mother-in-law came from both a gardening and an artistic background. Her mother left us a collection of watercolours from the 1930s of the walled Kitchen Garden as it was then, with a splendid herbaceous border and the highest eucalypts in Ireland (which have since blown down) towering over the garden wall. After my father-in-law's tragic death from tuberculosis, my mother-in-law kept the whole estate going. Six years later, in 1953, she married Ray Milner and together they restored the castle.

I have had such a dilemma since coming to live here. On the one hand, I have not wanted to spoil what is here or detract from its feeling of enclosed antiquity, yet, on the other hand, we have also been infected by the most virulent attack of the 'improvements' virus. Tom has built a rustic temple in the Kitchen Garden to protect a marble statue of a headless Andromeda chained to her rock. The hens live in a Gothic hen house, and pears, fig trees and clematis now line the noble grey stone walls. In the greenhouse, small black grapes flourish from vine cuttings given to my mother-in-law by Dick Charteris from Cahir Park, County Tipperary. A fuchsia hedge trims the orchard and a lovely semi-circular garden seat was given to us by the nuns when they left their convent near Mount Trenchard. The bees only take offence if one stands directly in their flightpath in front of one of the hives.

The small Gothic Hermitage slowly reappeared after much digging, clearing and drying out until a pebble floor was revealed under a brick-vaulted coved ceiling. Ferns, Solomon's seal and oak trees have been planted all around, with clouds of windflowers which are closely followed by primroses. A Woodland Walk has been created, its beginning marked by a wave of wild garlic. Across the stream, you turn up a small incline past conifers and specimen trees until you reach a stunning view over the steel ribbon of the Shannon. Shrubs are planted to see if they can withstand the west winds and an octagonal thatched Gothic shelter and seat are planned. Every year trees are blown down and much agonizing goes on about what to plant instead. 'We are very vulnerable to experts here,' Tom sighed plaintively a few winters ago, as we argued our way around the Pleasure Grounds wondering whether to plant a maze or a boxwood edging around the castle or have clipped yews marching up the central path. In the end we have done nothing, perhaps because we know that the garden we already have is the most precious of all.

*Plan of Glin Castle*

1. Gothic Entrance
2. Woodland Walk
3. Standing Stones
4. Hermitage
5. Kitchen Garden
6. Yew Avenue
7. Edwardian Seat & Pond
8. Rustic Temple
9. Old Farmyard
10. Stables
11. Gothic Lodge
12. River Shannon

# ILNACULLIN
## COUNTY CORK

Ilnacullin ('Island of the Holly') is the name of a garden which is also known as Garinish or The Italian Garden, that was started in 1910 on an island in a beautiful inlet off Bantry Bay in County Cork. After leaving Killarney, the road dips and weaves past lakes, through tunnels and along the edge of cliffs, until finally you arrive at sea-level in Glengarriff.

The garden is reached by catching a ferry. There are frequent ferries leaving from three different jetties, the middle one of which must be the most romantic quay – near a waterfall surrounded by islands just a short distance off the main street of the village. Stepping onto the boat, the outer world seems to recede. Removed from reality, it is as though you are playing a part in a play, as the boat slowly chugs out into the middle of the watery theatre. The lime-green hills and mountainous peaks around you act as your auditorium, lakes glint in the folds of rocky precipices and little ferries criss-cross the ocean.

Seals wait languorously, like mermaids, for the tide to rise and float them off their seaweed-draped rocks, and a heron, disdainful and alert at his post, scorns even to look in your direction. You begin to get an idea of what it must have been like nearly a hundred years ago, and what it was that prompted the beautiful Violet le Strange to tell her cousin Constance Markievicz that she had to live here. She had recently married John Annan Bryce MP, and was sailing past the barren island after she had spent the summer at Glengarriff Castle.

It was such a peculiar idea at the time to suddenly attempt to create a garden on a completely barren island in the middle of the bay. Could it have been just a whim on their part, or was there more to the Bryces' plan to create a microclimate on what has become almost a botanical Noah's Ark? Could it have been the miraculous ecological re-colonization of the island of Krakatoa after the stupendous eruption of its volcano in 1883 when it was reduced to a barren lunar landscape? Annan Bryce had spent time in the Far East and was a member of the National Geographic Society and thus would have known all about this event. Or could they have gained inspiration from a visit to the lush plantings of the Borromeo Gardens on Isola Madre, which had been a bare rocky island in the middle of Lake Como in Italy surrounded by mountain ranges? Although there is no evidence that either of the couple visited the gardens on Isola Madre, it is possible that they both did. It is a question which specialists who are interested in the garden often debate. There are no solid clues left, and today we can only speculate.

In 1910, the island of Ilnacullin belonged to the British War Office. The only structure here was a Martello Tower which had been built in 1800 in the anticipation of having to fend off an invasion by Napoleon. Therefore, the Bryces bought the island, tower and all. They soon realized that their prize would be continually buffeted and swept by Atlantic gales, and they began the task of blasting the rock and bringing over top soil and humus from the mainland to boost the existing thin, shallow and peaty soil. The fundamentals of establishing shelter were well understood in Ireland at that time, and the Royal Dublin Society awarded premiums for the planting of shelter belts. A thick coniferous fringe around the outer edge of the island was soon in place to ward off the storms.

The Bryces commissioned Harold Peto, the eminent English architect-turned-landscape designer known for his work at Iford Manor in Wiltshire and in the south of France, to build their mansion and lay out the garden. Harold had a great love for Italy. Perhaps, looking out over Bantry Bay, he was reminded of the Bay of Naples or even Vesuvius. Maybe he was inspired by the paintings of Veronese (1528–1588), in which the landscape is seen almost through a frame. It is possible that the inspiration for the Ionic

*Above: Temple of the Winds, a viewing terrace from which you can see across the water to the bare heather-covered old, red, sandstone peaks of the Caha Mountains.*

*Opposite: The island of Ilnacullin lies snugly in the shelter of the hills of Cork and Kerry.*

*Above: The clock tower at the corner of the Walled Garden is all that is visible on Ilnacullin when one looks down from the Martello Tower. The pine trees and cypresses provide the essential shelter belt for the hidden garden.*

*Opposite above: There are many different varieties of angel's trumpets – this one with red and yellow flowers blooms in the late summer at Ilnacullin.*

*Opposite below: The entrance to the Walled Garden, framed by an evergreen large-leaved magnolia and a fuchsia in full bloom.*

order for the capitols and the use of different-coloured marbles for the pillars came from the Villa Giulia in Rome. Indeed, the enclosed and sunken gardens of which you can see the remains in Pompeii and Herculaneum would have been noble precedents for the garden at Ilnaculin.

In spite of Edith Wharton's warning in *Italian Villas and Their Gardens*, published in 1904, that 'a marble sarcophagus and 12 twisted columns will not make an Italian garden', Annan Bryce accepted Peto's architectural plans, although he did not like his horticultural ones. Being a plantsman himself, Annan took over the planning and gathering of the plants, so that patron and architect worked harmoniously together. They employed 100 men for three years before the outbreak of the First World War. The vast mansion of five storeys to have been built near the Martello Tower was never completed. Instead, the gardener's cottage was enlarged and it was here that the artist Æ (George Russell) and George Bernard Shaw, the author and playwright, would sometimes come and stay. It was also where the legendary Scottish head gardener, Murdo Mackenzie, eventually lived.

Four years after the death of Annan Bryce in 1924, Murdo came to look after the garden with Annan's widow and son Rowland. The garden that we see today is largely the work of this genial and knowldgeable Scot. After his retirement 50 years later, he would take people around the island using a marvellous Scottish weeding tool as a walking stick with which he rooted out any weeds that caught his eye. These weeds included millions of seedlings of *Griselinia littoralis* planted for shelter in bygone days. One day Murdo spotted a variegated leaf among all the green ones. He carefully cut away all the green shoots, leaving the variegated one so that slowly the sport asserted itself. This original plant is now a tree and *Griselinia littoralis* 'Bantry Bay' with its custard-and-green leaves is a tender plant to be cherished.

The initial Italianate ideas for the planting were not very successful. The Bryces quickly understood that the landscape had to be invented first in order to create a mellow microclimate, and to complete the envisioned planting, they needed to gather plants from all four corners of the earth. The result is a layout in which a disciplined compartmented architectural framework, whose walls provide support against which the shrubs can be trained and supported, is combined with glorious sweeps of untrammelled Robinsonian plantings.

The view of the lily pond and steps leading up to the pavilions of the Italian Garden is well known, with wisteria twining around the Bath stone loggia and dwarf bonsai in pots. The crumpled larch is said to be 300 years old. There is a drowsy aura on the flagged terrace and it gets intensely hot in summer. Because of the moisture and humidity everything grows faster than in other parts of Ireland, which gives the impression that the plants and trees on the island are more mature than they really are.

The raised beds around the terrace are filled with treasures such as Australian bottle brushes, including the crimson *Callistemon salignus* 'Murdo Mackenzie', several different Indian mallows, including *Abutilon* 'Ashford Red' and 'Cloth of Gold', and the enchanting tiny-leaved netting plant (*Corokia*) hung with the deep purple- and blue-flowered *Clematis* x *durandii*, a hybrid from France that has no tendrils and therefore needs support. The New Zealand tea trees (*Leptospermum*) are splashed with pink or white flowers in late spring and early summer and have to be protected by timber frames and sacking during frosty winter nights. The dwarf tea trees called 'Kiwi' are planted in pots and the crushed leaves smell delicious, and there is also a very rare tea tree with bicoloured petals of pink and white called 'Rowland Bryce', which was given to the owner of Treseders Nursery in Cornwall by Murdo, and introduced by them in the early 1970s. An angel's trumpet (*Brugmansia sanguinea*) growing in a terrace bed with its yellow petals edged in red seems to be perfectly hardy, although on the mainland it would never survive outside a greenhouse. Among many others that would usually live indoors, the delicate white, scented *Rhododendron* 'Lady Alice Fitzwilliam' lives happily on the terrace all year round. The *Lophomyrtus bullata* from New Zealand has polished quilted leaves. The unusual *Pseudowintera colorata*, which rarely grows to more than 1m (3ft), has already reached 7m (23ft), but this seems quite mundane compared with the shining greenery of its relative *Drimys winteri*. Just breathing the air in this enclosure makes you feel that you are in a different and magically charged atmosphere.

The craggy bastions that rise up from the hillsides are smothered with rambling roses, carefully trained and pinned across the face of the rocks. Walking along the path that leads through the trees and shrubs, you emerge

at the Happy Valley with its roofless Greek temple at one end overlooking the water, and the Martello Tower at the other, joined by swathes of planting on both sides of the *tapis vert* that stretches between them. This glade embodies the paradise garden as described by William Robinson, in which a whole range of exotic plants from all the continents of the world are brought together and planted to make it seem as if they had all occurred there naturally. An avenue of Italian cypresses leads to the temple, and then along the sides of the glade are dawn redwoods (*Metasequoia glyptostroboides*), gum trees, the Huon pine (*Lagarostrobue*) from Tasmania and the native silver birch. The yellow-flowered *Rhododendron macabeaum* from India is a giant compared with the Japanese species *Rhododendron yakushimanum* whose young growth is wrapped in delicate felt covering in winter. Southern hemisphere trees, such as the Kauri pine (*Agathis australis*) from New Zealand and the blazing Chilean fire-bush (*Embothrium coccineum*) mingle with northern shrubs such as azaleas, dogwoods and lily-of-the-valley bushes (*Pieris*), as well as other southerners, such as daisy bushes from New Zealand, *Eucryphia* and mimosa.

Passing by the Bog Garden, where the pickerel weed with a long stalk and blue flower is growing out from under the water, and walking up the steps towards the Martello Tower, you come to the Viewing Point, which looks across the bay to other islands over the mussel beds and lobster pots. Your ears are filled with the sound of the sea. On the downward path, there

*Opposite: The Pavilion is a shady place, curtained by wisteria. The cream stone used came from England*

*Below: The cool pillared loggia of the Pavilion, built of Portland stone, offers shelter from the weather in this island garden and was the centre-piece in Harold Peto's garden plan.*

*Above: Harold Peto's splendid Pavilion is the centre-piece of the garden at Ilnacullin. The main house that he planned was never built. The Pavilion is wreathed with wisteria and there is a border of phlox beneath the balustrades.*

is a Monterey pine, blown down in the storm of Christmas 1998 when a whirlwind swept through the shelter belts, and destroyed 64 trees. The enormous root system of this tree is laced across the bare rock and clings to the shallow sandy soil around the edge.

You can seek refuge from the windy hill in the sheltered Walled Garden. Its grey stone pedimented gate has jasmine which climbs through the ironwork of the fanlight. Through the gate and the jasmine you can see beyond to the soft, lush herbaceous borders that stretch the whole length of the middle of the garden, bringing back memories of those long golden summer afternoons between the two world wars. The stone walls are dripping with clematis, wisteria and vines, while hydrangeas, lilies, hoherias, apple trees, cherries, magnolias, roses and camellias are all in a beautiful tangle in the different sections, and the *Michelia doltsopa*, a white-blossomed cousin of the magnolias from the Himalayas and China, grows against a wall next to a marble Roman sarcophagus. There is an attractive little

*Above: Hydrangeas are one of the most common plants throughout southwest Ireland.*

summerhouse with a pointed roof at one corner and clocktower at another. You emerge onto a gravel terrace and a green lawn that was once the lawn-tennis court with the wisteria-clad loggia ahead of you.

Everywhere there are miraculous things growing, the America bull bay (*Magnolia grandiflora*) and *M. delavayi* from China, *Viburnum tomentosum* in elegant layers, a blue cedar of Lebanon, mixed fuchsias, yuccas, myrtles, and hoherias in late summer. In late spring, there is the wisteria on the stone loggia with *Phlox paniculata* beneath, and in early summer Livingstone daisies scramble across the rocks. Nothing goes to waste on the island at Ilnacullin. Compost is made to enrich the soil using seaweed, light prunings, leaves and grass cuttings. The planting is ongoing in the mature gardens. However, because the conditions are constantly changing behind the shelter belts, so the garden is continually being redesigned, as though by the very plants and trees themselves. Before 1910 Ilnacullin was simply a bare and rocky island. Now it is often compared with the Garden of Eden.

# KILFANE GLEN & WATERFALL
## COUNTY KILKENNY

The story of how the gardens at the Kilfane Waterfall were lost, rediscovered and carefully restored by Susan and Nicholas Mosse would easily fill several chapters of a novel. When the Mosses first came to live in the Kilfane Dower House in the late 1980s, the garden was surrounded by impenetrable woods of *Rhododendron ponticum* and laurel. Ever since, they have worked unceasingly to cut back the encroaching jungle, and the garden that has emerged is a fascinating juxtaposition of two distinct parts.

At first glance, the upper section of the garden seems to fit into a fairly conventional layout of different compartments around the small red Dower House that was once part of the Kilfane demesne. Roses and jasmine climb up a stone barn. The lawn at the back of the house is home to a spreading oak. Mature trees, the stone pond and pergola, and trimmed-back laurel hedges, which had been part of a Victorian garden, have been rescued from the invading forest.

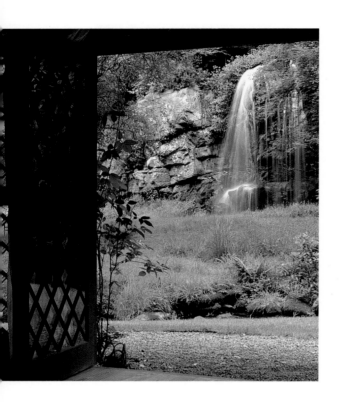

Herbaceous borders and the Moon Garden have been planted in compartments. At the front of the house, a vista has been cut through the surrounding woods showing the distant hill of *Sliabh na mBan* and a glade planted with ornamental grasses. The glade leads to William Pye's smoothly flowing fountain, where the water runs away down a goblet-shaped funnel in a bronze drum. It is then that you realize that this section of the garden is not a mere recreation of a Victorian garden in the style of Sissinghurst, but a cleverly laid-out sculpture garden. Modern sculptures, each one specially made for a particular site, confront and surprise you at each and every turn.

The second part of this garden story is the romantic tale of the rediscovery and restoration of a ruined *cottage ornée*, once a popular feature of eighteenth-century gardens. Discovered deep in a woodland glen at the foot of an artificial waterfall on a tributary of the River Nore, the Mosses have not only restored the cottage to its former glory, but also created around it a beautiful woodland garden

The entrance to Kilfane Waterfall Garden is marked by a frog-inhabited pond edged with arum lilies, iris and the giant Tibetan cowslip (*Primula florindae*). Through dappled birch and oak woods, carpeted with shuttlecock ferns and mosses, a little bridle path takes you to the old orchard, passing the mysterious sculptures that appear to be growing out of the trees. Dry-stone walls enclose two sides of the orchard, and a hedge of white *Rosa rugosa* runs its length. Circles of crab apple trees are planted in the grass facing a border, which in spring is swept by drifts of indigo grape hyacinths, and in summer is filled with blue-flowered delphiniums, campanulas and lobelias.

The square pool in the next compartment is edged with granite taken from the old Kilkenny railway platform. Water lilies and golden orfes inhabit the pool. Stone troughs are filled with Jerusalem sage (*Salvia sclarea turkestanica*), and a wooden pergola is loaded with clematis and two white roses, 'The Garland' and *Rosa mulliganii*, which is named after the late Dr Brian Mulligan, the Belfast-born horticulturist, who became Director of the University of Washington Arboretum in Seattle.

Next you walk down into the white Moon Garden, entirely enclosed within laurel hedges. Here there are white flowers, such as cosmos, delphiniums, libertia, daisies, campanulas, arum lilies, roses, clematis and mock orange, which are complemented by the rivers of the silver-leaved lamb's lugs (*Stachys byzantina*) and crisp green boxwood obelisks. The long, narrow laurel-hedged Victorian fern path comes to an end in a wooden-framed, full-length concave mirror that elegantly distorts the image, while reflecting the long green hedges that seem to stretch on and on to infinity along several avenues behind you.

Another winding path leads temptingly downwards, through holly and ivy, and towards the sound of rushing water. The woodland clearings are thickly planted with yellow columbines, Solomon's seal (*Polygonatum*), ferns, hardy geraniums, dicentras and foxgloves. As you descend still further, the path turns sharply and you can see the valley filled with towering trees. Finally, a rustic stone bridge crosses the river and here steps lead up through the woodland, past gnarled roots, mossy tree trunks and arching sprays of laurel. The tops of the sweet chestnuts are just visible on the other bank of the river through the laurel-hung path.

Then, quite unexpectedly, you come across the overhanging roof of a thatched cottage on a smooth green sward. A spiral staircase leads down to the river, and old roses are enclosed in a criss-cross fence. You can take tea sitting on rustic chairs, looking on to a waterfall falling from the cliff on the opposite bank. A single red rose drapes the cottage and honeysuckle, jasmine and clematis twine through the trellis. Great boulders are carpeted with mosses and cloaked with plants. Some of the boulders have been made into a seat, where you can sit and gaze across the river at the cottage. To reach the waterfall, cross the bridge and follow the stone steps that wind through the forest back up the hill.

The big house at Kilfane is 3km (2 miles) along the road and both gardens were once part of its demesne. The house still stands in the middle of its landscaped park (not open to the public) surrounded by majestic trees. A purple beech, sweet chestnuts and giant redwoods are part of the planting and a Folly opposite the house stands in the middle of a dried-up lake. The early-nineteenth-century Protestant church tower is another eye-catcher and was used as a marker in point-to-point races in the days of the Kilkenny Hunt.

The Walled Garden of the big house is entered by an elaborate wrought-iron Gothic gate, which leads through further Gothic trellised arches that are linked by little chains and support climbing roses. These are surrounded by overgrown old apple trees, Irish yews and thick box hedges.

In the 1790s two brothers, John and Richard Power, lived at Kilfane. They used to enjoy taking their guests on the 3km (2 mile) walk or donkey ride to see the waterfall and eat supper in the *cottage ornée*. It was all part of the romantic ideal that linked a group of people who lived around Kilkenny in the late-eighteenth and early-nineteenth centuries. John started the Kilkenny Hunt in 1797, and Richard started the Kilkenny Theatre in 1802, which gave performances in aid of charity for a season every year for nearly 20 years. They were resident landlords, as were their neighbours and friends the Wrixon-Bechers, who lived at Creagh in West Cork but also had a house at Ballyglibin near Kilkenny. Other neighbouring families included the Tighes at Woodstock, the Bushes at Kilmurray, and the Trenches at Heywood.

After the Union between Ireland and England in 1800, when most landlords became absentee and migrated towards the grand life in London, this particular group of cultivated and patriotic individuals determined to stay in their demesnes. They improved their estates and threw all their energies into creating a provincial society in Kilkenny that would rival that of Bath, in England, a particularly fashionable area at that time.

During the theatre season, people would flock down from Dublin to go to the play by night and to hunt by day. The actors were the gentlemen from the neighbouring houses and their guests, and the ladies were professional actresses. Several of the actresses later married their leading men, Bessy Dike marrying the poet Thomas Moore, and the great beauty and famous actress Eliza O'Neil marrying William Wrixon-Becher of Creagh in the church at Kilfane. Half the guests at the wedding wore hunting clothes and the rest wore their theatrical fancy dress!

Thomas Moore acted at Kilfane, where plays were often put on in the big house. He was staying at Jenkinstown House for the Kilkenny theatre season in the October of about 1805, where he saw a *Rosa chinensis* 'Old Blush' still in bloom, which, it is said, inspired him to write his love-lorn ballad 'The Last Rose of Summer'. At the beginning of the 1800s, European gardeners did not have a wide choice of roses, and in particular they did not have many that would blossom throughout the summer into autumn and even, in mild years, into winter. The rose that Thomas Moore saw came to Europe from China in 1789, a derivative of two wild Chinese species, the true Chinese rose (*Rosa chinensis*) and the tea rose (*Rosa gigantea*). This new import had the ability to blossom in the Irish climate from late spring to mid autumn, and when cross-bred with other roses passed on this remarkable characteristic. Today, a direct descendant of this same Jenkinstown House old China rose 'Old Blush' is flowering in the National Botanic Garden in Glasnevin.

It was John Power's wife, Harriet, the niece of Henry Grattan who landscaped these gardens. She had written a poem about two other gardens that she had already designed at Mount Juliet, the home of the Earls of Carrick, and at Gurteen, where one of her daughters lived. Harriet created the *cottage ornée* and devised the planting of the surrounding glen. The cottage would probably have been used most between the 1790s and 1820s, after which the Powers visited it less and less often. Finally, left to its own devices, the area was overtaken by the forest and completely forgotten. In 1988, no one alive had ever heard of the cottage or garden. The big house was still there, and what had been the Kilfane Dower House in the middle of a wood was for sale.

Nicholas Mosse, the famous potter from nearby Bennettsbridge, and his American wife, Susan, came to look at it, and, having seen the house, went to walk around the woods and immediately fell in love with the place. They bought the house and started work on the upper section of the garden, having no idea at the time that the second part existed. But when Jeremy Williams, the architect, came to dinner in 1990 and told them that he had seen watercolours in the Royal Society of Antiquaries of Ireland of a *cottage ornée* and waterfall, they determined to find and restore them. They began to explore, hacking back the laurels, and almost at once they found paths.

*Opposite top: A distorting concave mirror called 'Faeries Gate', made in 1995 by Sean Mulcahy, creates the illusion that the long narrow Victorian fern-edged path stretches away to infinity.*

*Opposite bottom: 'Descending Vessel Kilfane' made by David Nash in 1996 is a piece of sculpture in which a pointed arrow appears to be coming up out of a tree. This was specially commissioned by Susan Mosse.*

*Below: This hypnotically comtemplative water sculpture called 'Vessel' is by William Pye. Installed in 1998, it stands in a glade near the house.*

*Bottom: If you tap the outside of the bronze drum of the 'Vessel' that contains the water, the ripples spiral across the surface before plunging down smoothly into the goblet of the central funnel.*

Gradually a flight of stone steps emerged, leading down into the chasm through which the river flowed, cascading from pool to pool along the glen. This is the same river that had to fill the big pond at Kilmurry (home of the incorruptible Charles Kendal Bushe in the eighteenth century, and where the garden painter Mildred Anne Butler lived at the end of the nineteenth century), and the ornamental lake in the garden at Kilfane. And then, having stumbled across the river, they came upon heaps of stones and two walls with laurel growing out of the stonework, with the remains of a porch standing where the cottage had been in the painting. When Nick found the ornamental pebblework pavement that runs around the edge of the cottage, he knew that he had uncovered the footprint of the building. Using the watercolours as reference, the Mosses gradually restored the cottage.

It seemed at first as though the waterfall had completely vanished, However, shortly afterwards the Mosses discovered the dried-up canal that had been built in the 1790s to create the waterfall, diverting the stream for a mile and allowing the water to tumble over the cliff beside the cottage. Not only had Harriet Power conceived the cottage, she must also have envisioned that it needed a waterfall to complete the romantic landscape. While the Powers owned all the required land for their Romantic garden, it took the Mosses protracted negotiations over several years to buy the land and restore the canal to its original function, which was quite a feat of engineering even today, let alone nearly 200 years ago.

This restored *cottage ornée* is the oldest one of its kind in Ireland and, as with the Swiss Cottage at Cahir Park, was copied from the ideas of the French Queen, Marie Antoinette. Bored with the formalities and the routine of the French Court, she had the idea of building a country village where she and her friends could play at living in simple rusticity. The Queen's fantasy of rural life, called 'Le Hameau', was built in the grounds of the Petit Trianon at Versailles. All the buildings were thatched, and the outer walls covered in trellis and must have been the direct inspiration for these beautiful Irish cottages. Maybe the Kilfane cottage inspired the world-famous Ladies of Llangollen, Lady Eleanor Butler and Miss Sarah Ponsonby, who escaped from the grandeur of their unhappy homes near Kilfane to live together in a rural idyll in a cottage in Wales.

This romantic garden, with its waterfall and restored garden building, is of particular Irish interest historically, as it sheds light on the lives of a group of gifted and artistic people in the late-eighteenth and early-nineteenth century – men and women, who were all, in one way or another, to play an important part in the cultural and intellectual life of their country. The discovery of Harriet Power as an unsung eighteen-century garden designer, and the replanting of the glen and restoration of the *cottage ornée* are perfect examples of the stories Kilfane has to tell. These, combined with the Mosses' twentieth-century vision of their atmospheric plant and sculpture garden melting into the surrounding wild woods of Kilfane, brings this lost romantic garden, with a long, albeit fractured history, to life again.

*Plan of Kilfane Glen and Waterfall*

1. Grotto
2. Waterfall
3. Rustic Bridge
4. Stream Nore
5. Cottage Ornée
6. Mr Butler's Bridge
7. Pine Island
8. Stone Steps to Valley
9. Steps to Cockpit

# KILLRUDDERY
## COUNTY WICKLOW

The approach to Killruddery through a row of modern houses offers no clue that you are about to enter the most complete seventeenth-century garden in Ireland, and one of the most important surviving gardens of its type in the whole of England and Ireland. Set among the romantic peaks of the Large and Small Sugar Loaf Mountains in County Wicklow, Killruddery has always been known as the 'Big House' of the busy seaside town of Bray. In 1618, it was granted to the Norman-English Sir William Brabazon (later the first Earl of Meath). His grandson Edward, the 4th Earl, as part of the newly rich colonial aristocracy, was an enthusiastic follower of fashions – and this extended to his gardens. After the devastation caused by the Civil War, Ireland looked to France (where the monarchy had just been restored) for inspiration. In 1684, the fourth Earl employed a noted French gardener, Monsieur Bonet, who was inspired by King Louis XIV's garden designer, Andre Le Nôtre, at Versailles.

The idea for the twin canals that stretch down the garden from the house at Killruddery came from Le Nôtre's canals at the Château de Courances, 50km (30 miles) south of Paris, and at Killruddery, these inky black *miroirs d'eaux* (water mirrors), measuring 180m (550ft) in length, were also used to stock fish for the house. There is no known English or Irish precedent for these canals, although the gardens at Antrim Castle, which were planted at the same time, contain a single canal which has just been restored.

The fourth Earl had obviously been gripped by gardening fever, as an advertisement published in 1711 highlighted Killruddery's new summerhouse and a 'pleasure garden, cherry garden, kitchen garden, New Garden, Wilderness, gravel walks and bowling green'. It also mentioned that the garden was walled, that it had many fruit trees and that the canals were full of carp and tench. In keeping with the spirit of the times, Killruddery constituted a physical expression of the fourth Earl's status and wealth, and was intended to dazzle and impress friends and rivals alike. It was conceived as a 'garden of entertainment', with different garden 'rooms' to be used as extensions of the house in the style of the English 'Elizabethan Renaissance'. A few features, such as the Ace of Clubs pond, have disappeared completely but the simple plan of the demesne which was drawn up between 1740–50 is still perfectly evident today.

> In Seventeen Hundred and Forty and Four,
> The Fifth of December … I think 'twas no more,
> At Five in the morning by most of our Clocks,
> We rode from Killruddery, to try for a Fox'.

*Previous page, main picture: A pensive statue gazes through the autumn leaves of the circular beech hedge that encloses the stone pond in the 'Wilderness'.*

*Previous page, detail: The leaves of the* Ginkgo biloba *or maidenhair tree which stands in a sheltered position within one of the Angles.*

So wrote Thomas Mozeen, a friend of the fourth Earl, and a well-known actor and keen huntsman, in his famous ballad 'The Killruddery Hunt' in 1744. The primitive oil painting (c. 1740) celebrating this hunt still hangs at Killruddery, depicting hounds and huntsmen streaming across the landscape, with the original house and garden layout showing the 'Angles'. These are shown on the painting, on the eastern side of the canals; the great radiating hedges of beech, hornbeam and yew which are planted in the shape of a *patte d'oie* (literally the 'foot of the goose').

Nearly a century later, during the 1820s, the tenth Earl, with his architects Richard Morrison and and his son William Vitruvius Morrison, turned the house around half-circle so that it now faces north, and changed it from the Caroline Killruddery that is seen in the hunting painting into a Jacobean-revival palace, of which a large part was pulled down in 1953.

The twin canals flank a central walkway, leading to a circular pond with a single jet of water. Further on, a narrow canal takes the same curve and then runs westward beyond the ha-ha, forming a break between the garden and what used to be the 4th Earl's deer park. The double Lime Avenue starts mid-way across the park and continues over the crown of the hill, while belts of beechwood on either side of the lime avenue rise up towards the slopes of the Small Sugar Loaf Mountain. The eastern side of the garden, which was bounded by the old road to Bray, is subdivided into three parts. One area used to have a maze, which is now gone, and another a bowling green, now planted with silver birch. The surviving Angles take up the third part. On the western side of the canals lies the Wilderness (a French *bosquet*) with the Sylvan Theatre and the Beech Pond Circle.

*Below left: Sheep graze in the old deer park beneath the majesty of the double Lime Avenue. A single jet from the fountain rises directly in line with the vista.*

*Below: Twin canals lead the eye into the landscape and add a touch of quietly formal serenity, reflecting green leaves against the pale blue sky.*

*Above: A bird's eye view of the house at Kilruddery embraced by the trees. The peak of the Small Sugar Loaf Mountain can be seen beneath the approaching cloud formation. The formal garden stretching away from the house is hinted at but enticingly hidden.*

Within the complicated formal design, it is fascinating to see how 300 years of growth have filled in and blurred, but never lost, the symmetry and straight lines of the original plan. Walking through the Angles of high clipped hedges of beech and hornbeam with beech sentinels at the end of each *allée*, and perimeter walls of yew at the end of each triangle, it is like being among the pieces of the most elegant puzzle. Statues stand at the intersections and there is a vista from each that is closed by an ancient tree, such as a huge holly or Scots pine. A cast-iron nymph signals one intersection, which looks on to the vivid green grass in one direction and to the black water of the canal in another. Each Angle offers peace and seclusion between the high hedges. Sometimes the Angles have just a single tree planted in the middle, a *Ginkgo biloba* or a huge *Euchryphia* x *nymansensis*.

*Above: These trees in the full glory of their autumn colour stand to the East of the house in the clearing below the rock. They are in front of where the Elizabethan entrance once was, before the house was turned round in the 1820s.*

On the eastern side, you meet a cage-like circle of giant yews with their branches meeting high above your head. The yew cloisters lead to what was once the bowling green, where specially selected and graded grasses were used to ensure the true roll of the ball. The sunken lawn was surrounded by high grass terraces where spectators could sit comfortably and view the progress of the game. From here you can walk up the hill which is to your left through the beech trees, to the top of the rocky outcrop that stands to the east of the house. Squirrels race over the grass banks, holly bushes grow among the rhododendron and the sun shines through the clouds of gnats under the chestnut trees. On the top of the rock where gorse and ferns flourish, you can see the house sheltered by a ring of surrounding hills in a tapestry of fields. The town of Bray stretches away to the right.

In the mown grass clearing at the foot of the rock, there is a sprawling strawberry tree (*Arbutus unedo*), just as at home here as in its native haunts around the lakes of Killarney.

The receipts and plant lists – all in spidery handwriting – from the years after 1731 when the sixth Earl married Juliana Prendergast offer fascinating evidence of the history of the garden at this exciting time. The lists mention 31 different carnations bought from Mr Bacon in the first year. In other years there are 20 kinds of carnations, nearly 70 in another, and 42 in a third. In 1736, there were 74 Irish and 69 English varieties of auricula. There are also lists of ranunculus and tulips being shipped from Holland in 1739, tulips from Lille and Brussels in 1740, and hyacinths from Haarlem and Leyden in 1754. The garden must have been in its heyday at this time, as the flower books of the day testify. Indeed, some of Samuel Dixon's ravishing prints of flowers and birds were dedicated to the Countess of Meath. It is thought that, before gardening fashion banished all colour and flowers to the walled garden, there

*Below: The famous Kilruddery Angles with high hedges of yew, full grown limes, and an autumnal Venus bathed in the glory of the morning light.*

was a parterre linking the front of the house to the canals, and that many of these flowers were grown as bedding plants in between low box hedges. They would not have been planted in masses as in Victorian times, however, but rather as single specimens.

Juliana must often have wandered in the groves of the Wilderness thinking about her garden, and planning who would be coming to enjoy it. If she walked through the wood, she would have emerged facing a tall beech circular hedge with arched niches and clipped 'windows'. At the centre there is a round stone pond with a fountain. The hedge is formed from a double row of beech with a secret path through the middle. On an autumn day, with the crackle of the dry leaves underfoot and the eerie-looking entwined and tortured branches above, you feel as if you are walking through an illustration in a fairy story. The dying sun skirts over the russet leaves of the hedge and pierces the darkness of the wood, where a stricken gladiator on a plinth stands in a circle of ancient yews.

*Top: A nineteenth century cast-iron statue of an angelic beauty which the eleventh Earl of Meath bought and placed in the garden at some time in the 1850s or 60s.*

*Above: The glades and the clearings of the 'Wilderness' are peopled by statues. Here a cast iron goddess on her stone plinth appears at the corner at the joining of two paths seen through the dappled shade of bosky woodland.*

*Above: The fountains in the pond are stilled and golden beech leaves herald the approach of autumn, welcomed by the graceful nymphs that guard the pathway.*

By the 1820s, with the tenth Earl at Killruddery, the formal layout of the garden had come to be admired for its durability, with all visitors remarking on its antiquity. The tenth Earl bought and placed around the garden the cast-iron statues of gods and goddesses signed by Barbezat et Cie, Val D'Osne and F. Kahle of Potsdam. Near the Beech Pond Circle stands the most poetic of all auditoriums, the Sylvan Theatre, with its curved, shorn seats carved out of the banks of grass enclosed within a high bay laurel hedge. Moss-covered stone faces of comedy and tragedy lie on the ground as though waiting for the play to begin, and the tenth Earl wrote that 'acting had constantly taken place in this Sylvan Theatre, both in his, and his father's time, private theatricals being then much in vogue; dramatic parties were made up and then invited from one country house to another.' The idea much appealed to one visitor, Sir Walter Scott, who used it in *St Ronan's Well*. The theatre's grass banks give way to a lawn with a yew tree that is so old its bark looks like folds of material. Birdsong and the sound of a fountain nearby draw you towards the rose beds. A small Ornamental Victorian Dairy is smothered in clematis and a huge old *Magnolia grandiflora* spreads across the west-facing wall of the house.

In 1846, during the eleventh Earl's occupation of Killruddery, the garden was fully restored by the landscape gardener Daniel Robertson. A conservatory, designed by the architect William Burn, was built in 1852. It is said that the delicate lace-like stone parapet was copied from Lady Meath's tiara before it was sold to pay for the building work. Over the next century a rock garden was planted on an outcrop of rock to the east of the house and rose beds and hedges on a smaller scale were added near the Ornamental Victorian Dairy on the west. The gardens were kept in good order until a lack of gardening help after the Second World War meant that hedges and paths became overgrown.

In 1951, the Earl and Countess of Meath returned to live in Killruddery and were faced with an enormous house full of dry rot, heavy duties to pay and an overgrown garden. 'It was very gloomy,' remembers Lady Meath, 'the roof was leaking everywhere.' To start with, they decided to pull down one wing with the help of the architect Claude Phillimore. The former dining room with its view of the hill was made into a terrace, its decorative edging recycled from a dismantled gable.

When Lord and Lady Meath first came back to live here, they didn't have a gardener at all, and there were dandelions growing all over the walks. 'We beheaded them and poured sodium chlorate and would weed all around the long ponds with watering cans, and by degrees the paths came back. We grew raspberries and tried to sell the vegetables at market. We never stopped working in the summers.' For the first time, in autumn 1997, they were able to clip the Angles and now have two full-time gardeners who do the clipping once a year in winter.

The continued existence of the gardens at Killruddery is a tribute to all those who have been in charge of them over the years. They stand and flourish as testament to the planning and design skills of the 4th Earl, and the contrast between the man made formality of the gardens and the wild untamed sides of the Sugar Loaf Mountains, visible from all parts of the garden, is still as dramatic today as it would have seemed to him three centuries ago.

*Below: The playing fountains seen through the beech trees can only be heard when you are inside the circular hedge.*

*Plan of Killruddery*

1. Clock Tower
2. Ornamental Section
3. Beech Hedge Pond
4. Sylvan Theatre
5. Long Canals
6. Wilderness
7. The Angles
8. Round Pond with fountain
9. The Cascades
10. Lime Avenue

# MOUNT STEWART

## COUNTY DOWN

The house and gardens of Mount Stewart are situated on the edge
of Strangford Lough on the western shore of the narrow peninsula
of the Ards in County Down. The garden was created by Edith, Lady
Londonderry, a capricious lady of dauntless energy and enthusiasm, who
at first sight described her husband's ancestral mansion as being 'the
darkest, dampest, saddest place I ever stayed in'. Before long, though,
she was to transform the grounds into a whimsical and extravagant garden
reminiscent of a Lewis Carroll tale. The 80-acre site is characterized by
an almost overwhelming conglomeration of different styles of architecture
and planting, which is saved from confusion only by the sense that there
has been a single hand with a dashing touch at the helm throughout.
It is heartening to see that so much of what she created is still in such
good shape, with an extraordinary number of tender plants flourishing.

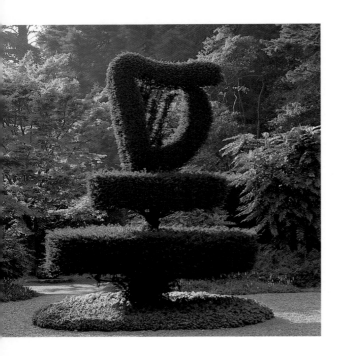

*Previous page, main picture: An arcade of closely clipped Leyland cypresses is one of the most unusual features in Mount Stewart, one of the jewels in the crown of the National Trust in Northern Ireland. Jerusalem sage and the grey, pointed foliage of* Kniphofia caulescens *complement each other, while a red-leaved cabbage palm stands aloof.*

*Previous page, detail: Nasturtiums planted in a stone trough provide a splash of colour.*

*Above: The harp is the emblem of Ireland. This one is formed from yew and stands within a shamrock-shaped compartment.*

When Lady Londonderry came to live here in 1919, she immediately swept away the holm oaks that made the house dark and airless, and launched a programme of non-stop planning, clearing, designing and planting that lasted from 1919 to 1927. Gertrude Jekyll sent over a plan for the Sunken Garden, and with this to hand Lady Londonderry set about reviewing all she knew about gardening and garden design. The Boboli Gardens in Florence, the Villa Gamberaia at Setignano, the Villa Farnese at Caparola, not to mention her mother's garden at Dunrobin Castle in Scotland, were all enthusiastically plundered for inspiration. The scale of the overall design and the intensity of the planting is awesome even today, and Lady Londonderry was assisted by a small army of builders and gardeners. It was during the difficult period of demobilization after the First World War, and landlords were being asked to employ as many extra people as possible. At least 20 men were allocated to Mount Stewart, and taking advantage of this opportunity, Lady Londonderry was able to forge ahead with her spectacular plans.

Realizing the benefits of the climate that the gardens enjoyed was key to their development. 'The really exciting and important thing about Mount Stewart was discovering the climate, and this, I think, I may claim to have done,' she wrote proudly. As Mount Stewart is situated in the northeast of Ireland, it has the major benefit of enjoying more sunshine and less rain than other parts of the country. It is also essentially frost-free. When Lady Londonderry started the garden, she had no idea that the Gulf Stream, which feeds the 27km (17 miles) long Strangford Lough, would make it possible for her to grow the many half-hardy shrubs and more tender *Rhododendron* species that one would usually expect to grow in a greenhouse. Mimosa trees, Banksian roses, the Chilean bell flower (*Lapageria rosea*) and countless other tender plants thrive happily out of doors. So narrow is the space between the head of Strangford Lough and that of Belfast Lough that Mount Stewart experiences island conditions – the atmosphere is humid and, in hot weather, there are very heavy dews at night. All these factors combine to bring about an extraordinary rate of growth, and throughout the garden the groves of eucalypts, rows of cabbage palms (*Cordyline australis*) and spiky-leaved palms create an atmosphere that you might expect to find in a garden in the Azores.

Two advisers encouraged Lady Londonderry to be adventurous and grow the tenderest plants: Sir John Ross-of-Bladensburg, who lived at Rostrevor in County Down amd made a marvellous collection of trees and rare shrubs from all over the world on the slopes of a hill overlooking Carlingford Lough, and Sir Herbert Maxwell of Montreith in Wigtownshire, who also had a wonderful garden packed with rare species. She also took advice from Gertrude Jekyll and corresponded with plant collectors Clarence Elliott, George Forrest and Frank Kingdon Ward. She ordered plants from nurseries across Europe, while her woody plant collection was dominated by southern-hemisphere species.

To cheer and enliven the surroundings of her husband's sober Georgian house, she threw out suites of garden rooms on the south, west and east fronts, all sheltered from the lough by a proscenium of trees. Without any view or vista through to the beautiful waters of the lough, Lady Londonderry succeeded in creating an enclosed, exotic and lush, almost dreamlike world.

Entering the garden on the west side, you walk through an ironwork gate flanked by stone pillars, with the sinuous necks of swans emerging from crowns, the family crest. The Sunken Garden was one of Lady Londonderry's first projects, and is surrounded on three sides by a tall clipped hedge of Leyland cypress, which is so feathery and such a bright green that it looks like a fur carpet. The heavy stone pergola is hung with potato vines (*Solanum*), clematis, fuchsias, California lilacs (*Ceanothus*) and *Rosa gigantea* from western China and northern Burma, as well as having uncommon and delicate slipperworts growing through the paved path below. Fifty-year-old bay trees, bought in Leghorn, are sculpted into domes and grown in pots on the terrace. Four herbaceous beds, carved out of the grass, are filled in summer with dephiniums, lilies, day lilies and phlox, and each is bordered by two different hedges meeting at the corners of tightly clipped boxwood and bay. Scattered throughout are tall tree heathers, *Erica arborea* and *E. lusitanica*, while in spring, borders of flame-coloured azaleas light up the greenery.

The journey through the gardens is compelling. Irresistible glimpses lead you from one compartment to the next, each one more enticing and exotic than the last. One of the most original compartments is designed in the shape

*Below: Roses and honeysuckles clamber up this stone-and-wood pergola. The splashes of scarlet are provided by nasturtiums and Peruvian lilies.*

*Above: The plant collection at Mount Stewart is outstanding. Here the red* Crocosmia masoniorum *is combined with the slender spires of white-flowered loosestrife.*

of a shamrock and surrounded by a 2m (7ft) hedge of English yew, with two scissor-clipped topiary crowns and topiary figures of a family hunting party chasing each other along the top of the hedge. The figures were copied and adapted from Queen Mary Tudor's fourteenth-century psalter. 'All the weird animals, devils, boats and birds are drawn in the margins of the leaves. All we did was substitute members of the family for the originals,' writes Lady Londonderry nonchalantly. The symbol of Ulster, a huge red hand, is planted in the gravel in *Begonia* 'Red Devil'. Behind this stands a yew tree clipped into flat, round table tops, on the topmost tier of which stands a topiary harp, the symbol of Ireland. The Londonderrys believe themselves to be descended from the first O'Neill, who, in a desperate race with a rival clan across the Irish Sea from Scotland, cut off his right hand and threw it onto Ulster's shore to lay claim to the country. Plants for winter interest grow in the beds behind this Celtic show-stopper: camellias, mahonias, sweet box (*Sarcococca*), *Viburnum* x *bodnantense*, and the graceful coral-stemmed Japanese maple, *Acer palmetum* 'Senkaki', There are also roses nearby, including 'Emily Gray' and 'Lady Hillingdon', tea trees from New Zealand (*Leptospermum scoparium*) and *Hydrangea involucrata* and *H. scandens* subsp *chinensis*.

The Lily Wood, next on the agenda, is in true Robinsonian style. A winding path leads past delicate rhododendrons, tree ferns over 3.5m (12ft) high, lots of lilies, such as *L. martagon* and 'Shuksan', the Chilean firebush

(*Embothrium coccineum*) from Rostrevor, eucryphia and various creepers growing up pine trees. There are blue poppies, primulas, hostas and trilliums, as well as the jealously prized *Cardiocrinum giganteum*, the stately Himalayan lily that reaches over 3m (10ft) and has huge white trumpet-shaped flowers.

From here, it is all too tempting to move straight into the Spanish Garden, but in order to realize the full extent of Lady Londonderry's vision, you should approach this garden from the front of the house with the Spanish-tiled loggia as your focus. The shape of the herbaceous beds in the centre of the adjacent Italian Garden, which runs the full length of the house, was copied from her mother's garden at Dunrobin Castle in Scotland. The inspiration for the accompanying stonework came from the Villas Gamberaia and Farnese. The high-clipped yew hedges of the Boboli Gardens were the idea for the rather more spindly version in Leyland cypress that frames the loggia. Pairs of columns are topped by heraldic griffins, urns and herms. Lady Londonderry did not approve of boxwood, so the beds are edged in a mixture of colours, using purple berberis, white heather, blue rue, golden thuja and silvery hebe. Two stone ponds filled with water lilies and surrounded by lilies and hostas are a complement to the surrounding beds of silvery mauve on the one side and a welcome alternative to the strong orange and reds on the other. Finally, there is a double row of New Zealand cabbage palms (*Cordyline australis*) marching down the middle.

*Above: Dodos guard Noah's Ark while griffins look on. The statuary at Mount Stewart is pure fun. And, true to the principles nurtured by Gertrude Jekyll (who helped Lady Londonderry design this garden), plant colours are carefully combined for maximum effect.*

*Above: A view of the main formal parterre at the south front of Mount Stewart. The dominant colours are 'hot' dark reds and oranges and yellows.*

*Opposite above: The centrepiece and focus of the front view from the house is the small Spanish tiled loggia in the Spanish Garden below the semi-circular flight of stone steps. The design of this garden was inspired by a plasterwork ceiling by Robert Adam that Lady Londonderry originally saw in the Mansion House in London.*

*Opposite below: Looking back from the Parterre to the terrace of the house itself across the fountain playing in the round stone pond. The walls of the house are hung with creepers, and the layout and shapes of the beds in the parterres were copied from those at Dunrobin Castle, Scotland.*

Lady Londonderry was not only a keen gardener, but also a famous political hostess. During the First World War, she had formed the Ark Club at Londonderry House, which provided an oasis in London for her family and close friends – soldiers, politicians, poets, artists and composers – to meet informally. The members of the club all took the names of animals alive or extinct, and many of them are represented on the Dodo Terrace, cast in concrete by a local craftsman in memory of the club. Lady Londonderry was Circe the Sorceress, Winston Churchill was Winston the Warlock, Ramsay MacDonald was Hamish the Hart, and so on. Four dodos on pillars guard the ark underneath the eucalypts, and other curious-looking creatures on their plinths along the walls eye the intruder with baleful half-human expressions.

The rhododendrons on the Dodo Terrace shelter the next compartment, which is the Mairi Garden, named after Lady Mairi Vane-Tempest-Stewart (later Viscountess Bury). It is planted in the shape of a Tudor rose and filled with blue and white plants, such as agapanthus, campanulas and *Galtonia candicans*, as well as white fuchsias, buddlejas and Bourbon roses. In the centre is a fountain dedicated to the 'Mary Mary Quite Contrary' of the nursery rhyme, as a reminder of the days when the youngest daughter of the house was put here to sleep in her pram next to the summerhouse and dovehouse. Wafts of resin fill the air from the 36m (120ft) *Eucalyptus globulus*, of which this garden has the most concentrated planting in northern Europe. They were grown from seeds brought back by Theresa Lady Londonderry from South Africa in 1894.

Although one could be excused for thinking that the tour was now over as a wisteria-covered tunnel leads to the carpark, in fact one would be missing the informal walks up into the slopes at the other side of the house. Here you can take the Lake Walk, passing the large artificial lake laid out in the 1840s. This is where you would have once looked down across an open park to the

house with the lough beyond. Now, on the path from the drive, there are
rhododendrons, azaleas, magnolias and a group of delicate *Cordyline indivisa*
from New Zealand, with their swordlike leaves. The banks of the lake are
decorated with Japanese ornaments collected by the Londonderrys on a tour
of Japan. Above the lake, you can see the distant turrets of the family burial
ground in a walled enclosure called in Irish 'Tir-n'an Og' or 'The Land
of the Ever Young'. The great white stag that is reputed to bear the souls
of the departed to heaven can be seen standing in a tree-lined glade.

Another path leads uphill through a wood of beech trees. Turning a
corner, in front of you stands a perfect copy of the Tower of Andronicus
Cyrrhestes in Athens. Built by the architect James 'Athenian' Stuart in 1780,
this is the Temple of The Winds, designed as a banqueting house and made of
pale Scrabo stone with floors of fir found in the bogs on the estate. It is
arguably the most beautiful garden building in Ulster. It gazes out serenely
over the blue waters of Strangford Lough, secure in its chastely perfect
proportions and untouched by the excitements of a later age.

Today, Mount Stewart is one of the most important gardens in Ireland.
It is the most complete example of the compartmental style of gardening
of its date in the country. Lady Londonderry died in 1959, but her daughter
Viscountess Bury still lives in the house, which along with the garden, now
belongs to and is cared for by the National Trust. Under the present Head
Gardener, Nigel Marshall, direct acquisition of seeds from America and
Australia has again become a vital part of the garden's regeneration. The plant
collection has expanded and been improved with new planting, thus keeping
Lady Londonderry's imaginative spirit alive.

*Plan of Mount Stewart*

1. Mairi Garden
2. Dodo Terrace
3. Fountain Walk
4. Spanish Garden
5. Italian Garden
6. Peace Garden
7. Lily Wood
8. River
9. Memorial Glade
10. Sunken Garden
11. Shamrock Garden
12. Lake Walk
13. Lake
14. The Hill
15. Temple of the Winds
16. Jubilee Avenue Walk
17. Rhododendron Wood
18. Ladies Walk

# MOUNT USHER
## COUNTY WICKLOW

Tucked into the landscape in between the hills of County Wicklow and the sea lie the gardens of Mount Usher. They are sheltered by the hills of the surrounding valley of the silvery River Vartry as it flows down from the Devil's Glen. When the famous eighteenth-century traveller and diarist Mrs Delany visited her friend Mrs Usher of Mount Usher in 1752, she reported on the beauty of the countryside. 'Fine meadows, shady lanes, one side skirted by mountains and hills of various shapes, diversified with cultured fields, bushes and rocks and some woods, on the other side a beautiful prospect of the sea and the roads like gravel walks, the hedges enriched with golden furze and silver May. This country is particularly famous for arbutus (the strawberry tree) and myrtles, which grow in common ground and flourish as in Cornwall.' One day they called on Mr Tighe, whose garden at his demesne Rossannagh was divided from Mr Usher's by 'a very pretty clear river: he came in his boat to waft us over'.

*Previous page, main picture:* Rhododendron barbatum, *a native of the Himalayas, is just one of the hundreds of rhododendrons which there are at Mount Usher, a garden in which the sound of running water is always present.*

*Previous page, detail:* Mahonia *make excellent winter-flowering shrubs. The genus is named after the Irish-American horticulturist Bernard McMahon.*

*Right: A happy combination – an azalea and some candelabra primulas blooming in spring.*

*Opposite: Scillas and daffodils form a carpet under* Acer griseum, *a splendid small maple renowned for its peeling cinnamon-red bark.*

When the Ushers of Mount Usher died or moved away, the Tighes must have bought up their property. Mr Tighe then leased it to a miller, who first ran a tuck mill for finishing woollen cloth and then a corn mill using the water from the river to turn the mill wheel. Time passed and, in the 1860s, Edward Walpole, a successful Dublin businessman involved in the linen trade, appeared on the scene. He was staying in Hunter's Hotel, a cream-coloured Georgian house that stands approximately 2km (1½ mile) from the garden. Edward and the owner of the mill, Sam Sutton, became fast friends, and he returned often to enjoy the mountain air and walk in the surrounding hills. Soon he was staying at the miller's house rather than the hotel, and had grown to love the wooded valley, so much so that when the miller's lease expired in 1868, Edward took it over. He acquired the 1 acre and 11 perches that began his family's relationship with Mount Usher, which was to last 112 years. He wasn't to know it immediately, but the site had almost perfect conditions for growing the tenderest of plants. The soil is alluvial gravel or sand overlaying patches of heavy clay and is lime free. The rainfall averages 90cm (36in) a year and frost is rare.

To start with, in place of the potatoes that grew in front of the house, Edward planted flowers and, to his astonishment, everything he planted flourished. He soon bought more land and enlarged the property. In 1875, when he was 77, Edward Walpole gave the property to his three sons. It was the combination of their skills that was to make Mount Usher into a perfect example of a Robinsonian garden. Edward and George were the gardeners, while Thomas, fascinated by civil engineering and architecture, was responsible for the planning of the waterworks and the bridges. They were succeeded by a grandson, E. Horace Walpole, one of the greatest Irish gardeners of his generation, and then, in turn, by his son Robert, who sold the property in 1980 to the present owner, Mrs Madeleine Jay.

The Walpole brothers filled the garden with a number of unusual plants little tried in Ireland before, collected from nurseries all over the world. Seeds and plants came from Britain, France, Italy and Germany, as well as New Zealand, Australia, Japan and North America. The original book of introductions still exists, with lists of plants bought from the Vilmorin Nurseries in France and from Yokohama in Japan.

In the early 1880s, William Robinson was firing his first salvoes against the stiff and formal Victorian ideal of planting in his book *The English Flower Garden*. He visited Mount Usher and gave his seal of approval. He thoroughly agreed with the way the Walpoles were mixing exotic plants with the native trees and shrubs, allowing nature and the natural habit of each plant to dictate its situation and planting. Frederick Moore, the Director of the Royal Botanic Gardens in Glasnevin, visited the brothers in 1885 and saw at once that Mount Usher had the perfect soil, water and climate to make an extraordinary garden. From then on, he kept them supplied with the names of new exotics, and helped them to collect the rare plants that otherwise would have been difficult to find in Britain or Ireland at that time.

*Above: The Vartry river is 'stepped' by weirs, creating a pattern of still water and white foam.*

Over the years, more land was bought and, in 1927, the freehold was purchased and the old mill pulled down. A modern house was then built around which the gardens have grown to the present 20 acre site. The philosophy, passion and knowledge of gardening, combined with a thorough understanding of the site and its conditions, were passed down through the generations of the Walpole family. Assistance was also provided by some of Ireland's leading horticulturalists. With the support of Mrs Jay, the present head gardener, John Anderson, who trained at the National Botanic Gardens and at the Royal Botanic Gardens at Kew, is continually collecting and planting very much in the Walpole tradition. Today, the ever-increasing collection of trees and plants at Mount Usher, where planting began in 1868, are all sited in a continuation of Robinsonian principles without a jarring note.

*Above: Sweet Gum tree with the last vestiges of its foliage, by the Vartry River.*

The mature trees that form the bones of the garden are truly awe-inspiring. Some were planted as early as the 1880s and they include the largest collection of southern-hemisphere conifers in the country – there are 28 species, from the New Zealand kauri pine (*Agathis australis*) to the Prince Albert's yew (*Saxegothea conspicua*) from South America. Northern conifers also thrive here. There are superb specimens of Montezumae's pine (*Pinus montezumae*) presented to Mount Usher in 1907 by Lord Wicklow, the handsome coffin juniper (*Juniperus recurva* var. *coxii*) from the China/Burma border, and Brewer's spruce (*Picea breweriana*) with its drooping branches.

Slender and graceful with their pale cream and grey trunks, the collection of Australian eucalypts contains about 50 different species, including the manna gum (*Eucalyptus viminalis*), the Tasmanian snow gum (*E. coccifera*), apple box (*E. bridgesiana*, formerly *E. stuartiana*) and alpine ash (*E. delegantensis*). There is also a comprehensive collection of southern beeches (*Nothofagus*), the most striking being the evergreens *N. menziesii*, the silver beech from New Zealand, and from Chile *N. nitida* (coigue de Chiloe) and *N. dombeyi* (coigue). In spring, the grass below is scattered with trout lilies and anemones, with fritillaries looking like small squares of checked muslin that have been dropped in the grass. In early spring, the flowers and buds make a startling impression on the bare wood of leafless trees and shrubs. The pure white flowers of *Magnolia salicifolia* seem like bands of folded linen against its bare branches and an early-flowering leafless cherry (*Prunus incisa*) has tiny flowers like pale pink shells. The Japanese magnolias, *M. kobus* and *M. obovata*, each have a brilliant central ruby boss of stamens, and *Primula megaseifolia* from the Black Sea coast of northern Turkey can be seen flourishing in a pocket on the river wall.

The River Vartry divides the garden, which is planted in long narrow strips along each of its banks. The engineering brother, Thomas Walpole, strung a series of bridges over the river, replacing the earlier stepping stones, and laid out the continuous trail of streams that weaves through the property. Ferns of every description grow on either side clinging to old tree trunks and stones.

When Mrs Jay bought the property, she banned the use of chemicals. John Anderson explains: 'Since we have stopped using them, we have got the thrushes and frogs back. In the autumn, the Vartry is full of herons, kingfishers, otters and wagtails, and sometimes 10lb salmon.' Rusty swamp cypresses (*Taxodium distinchum*), a Persian ironwood tree (*Parrotia persica*), Sweet Gum (*Liquidambar styraciflua*), Katsura tree (*Cercidiphyllum*

*Below: The maple walk leading to the banks of the Vartry River. Wild birds, such as these mallards, are especially encouraged at Mount Usher.*

*japonicum*), a golden larch (*Pseudolarix amabilis*), a New Zealand flax, mountain dogwood (*Cornus nuttallii*) and many more plants and trees lead the eye into the glades. Exotic plants have naturalized on the river banks, and myrtle, willow and giant Chilean rhubarb seem to be weeping into the water.

The Maple Walk is at its most brilliant in the autumn with the gleaming, curling bark of *Acer griseum*, the striated stems of snakebark maples and the red twigs of the coral-bark maple, *Acer palmatum* 'Senkaki'. Azaleas and rhododendrons supply colour in May, with *Rhododendron sinogrande* and *R. falconeri* flowering profusely, as well as the blue *R. augustinii* and the huge-flowered loderi hybrids. Through the summer and early autumn, the eucryphia collection is spectacular, with its large clumps and avenues of the special Mount Usher hybrid with large white flowers which is the result of a cross between *E. glutinosa* and *E. cordifolia*. Other summer delights are provided by *Hydrangea sargentiana*, *H. villosa* and golden hypericums, California lilacs (*Ceanothus*) and veronicas (*Hebe*). There are 20 acres of garden and perhaps 5,000 different plants. 2 per cent have come from South Africa, 50 per cent from Asia, the Himalayas and China, 8 per cent from Australasia, 8 per cent from Europe and 12 per cent from North America.

When Mount Usher was for sale, Mrs Jay bought the garden to save it. 'So many beautiful things in Ireland disappear and it would have been so awful if it had been lost,' she tells me, and feels that her daring has been rewarded many times over. John Anderson is tireless in his support, and has a vigilant eye and passion for plants. This managed wilderness, combining exotics and old native favourites, gives this garden a life and spirit that makes it a joy to visit at any time of the year.

*Below: The placid waters of the River Vartry reflect the glorious colours of graceful trees on a peaceful autumn afternoon.*

*Plan of Mount Usher*

1. Pond
2. Stream
3. Bridge
4. Old Millstone
5. Maple Walk
6. River Vartry
7. Azalea Walk
8. Bridge
9. Palm Walk
10. Nothofagus
11. Lime Walk

# NATIONAL BOTANIC GARDENS
## GLASNEVIN, DUBLIN

For over 200 years the National Botanic Gardens have been at the forefront of Irish horticultural progress. Arriving there today, you turn off the high street and pass through wrought-iron gates with two Georgian lodges, one on each side of the pathway. It is like entering a different world, leaving behind the streets of pink Victorian brick and the hustle and bustle of modern living. The feeling of being enveloped by a separate, yet demanding, discipline in a peaceful atmosphere is one to be savoured.

The Botanic Gardens were started in 1795 by Dr Walter Wade, a Dublin surgeon and male midwife. The successful petition to fund the gardens was manoeuvred through the Irish Parliament by the Speaker of the day, John Foster, himself a keen collector of plants, agricultural improver and tree planter at his estate, Collon in County Louth. He was also a leading light in the Royal Dublin Society, which was to manage the garden with a grant from the government.

There had been previous pleas to the government that the country needed a botanical garden for growing and studying medicinal plants, and also so that plants used in agriculture and horticulture could be promoted and improved.

So, 27 acres were purchased in Glasnevin, the Dublin suburb, with the River Tolka forming the northern boundary. Delville, the idyllic garden that had belonged to Dean Delany and his wife Mary, was nearby. Dean Delany had been a friend of the poet Thomas Tickell, the previous owner of the land, and it is said that Tickell had planted the old Yew Walk that still stands today in memory of his friend, the English essayist, Joseph Addison. It is this tangible connection with the past through its buildings, plants and trees that gives the Botanic Gardens such an atmosphere of tranquillity and romance.

Dr Wade was elected the Dublin Society's Professor of Botany in 1796. Two years later, John Underwood became Head Gardener at the Botanic Gardens, and for the next 25 years, until Dr Wade's death, they developed the basis of the plant collections. Standards then declined until Ninian Niven, a skilled gardener and designer, took over from Underwood in 1834. During his four years at Glasnevin, Niven breathed new life into the Gardens and was particularly interested in introducing new plants from overseas.

In 1838, David Moore was appointed Curator, and under his direction the Botanic Gardens became world renowned, with Queen Victoria giving her seal of approval by visiting the Gardens in 1849. Between 1843 and 1870 the great Curvilinear Range of glasshouses was built, making it possible for tender exotics to flourish. In 1845, orchid seed germinated for the first time in Glasnevin; the late blight of the potato was ominously observed on 20 August of the same year. In 1854, the Aquatic House was erected to house the giant water lily (*Victoria amazonica*) from the Amazon. The first hybrid pitcher plants (*Sarracenia*) were raised around 1870. David Moore died in 1879 and was succeeded by his son Frederick. Frederick Moore continued his father's excellent work, expanding the orchid and cycad collections, as well as continuing with the hybrid pitcher-plant breeding programme. Under his direction the Gardens gained a reputation for cultivating 'difficult' plants, and Glasnevin was considered superior to its sister botanic gardens at Kew and Edinburgh. Sir Frederick Moore and his wife Phylis were the undisputed king and queen of Irish horticulture. He retired in 1922 and was followed by several excellent Curators, who consolidated his work and added to the collections with hardy trees and shrubs being introduced from the Far East.

Donal Synnott, who has worked at the institution for 28 years, is the present Director and the Gardens are undergoing a renaissance under the guardianship of Dúchas, the Department of Arts, Heritage, Gaeltacht and the Islands. Donal feels that the Gardens at the moment are an under-utilized asset and is keen to bring them to a wider audience and, in particular, to encourage more Irish people to enjoy this great treasure.

As you enter the Botanic Gardens, you will see, at any time of day, gardeners tending the herbaceous borders. Here, as in the rest of the Gardens, Irish plants and trees are all carefully labelled with their Latin, English and Irish names. Plants and trees stand singly or in family groups or beds, allowing previously unmade connections to become clear. On my visit, I was surprised to discover that columbines and delphiniums belong to the same family.

Ahead of you is the elegant Victorian Curvilinear Range of greenhouses designed and built by Richard Turner between 1843 and 1868, now restored to their original glory by the Office of Public Works architect Ciaran O'Connor. The sun gleams on the small, thin, curved panes of glass, which fit into their cream-painted, graceful wrought-iron casing with classical pillars and Victorian frill. Within, the cycads look mysterious in their pots beneath the arching spandrels of the roof in the vapour of a simulated tropical downpour.

To the right of the Curvilinear Range stand the Cactus and Fern Houses. Outside, the structures are ringed by arum lilies (*Zantedeschia aethiopica*), agapanthus and libertia, and the lovely long-stemmed white bells of *Watsonia borbonica* subsp. *ardernei* from Cape Province in South Africa. The dry air of the Cactus House gives way to the dripping fernery in the Aquatic House, where the Jeremy Fisher-like, flat-cupped water-lily leaves of *Victoria amazonica* astonished the world when they were first shown in public in 1854. Ferns of every description line the artificial river gorge like a fairy grotto. The 400-year-old fern from the Royal Botanic Gardens in Melbourne that was presented to Trinity College, Dublin, in 1892 and then passed on to Glasnevin in 1969 looks completely at home among so many compatriots.

Today, the Great Palm House is sadly in need of repair. It was built in 1884 at a cost of £800 and in great haste, because the previous house was so rickety it was virtually blown down in gales. The paint is peeling and the

*Top: The handsome front entrance to the Great Curvilinear Range of cast iron glasshouses with a tropical mist being simulated within.*

*Above: Modern technology now provides a fog-like mist so that plants from tropical rainforests can be cultivated in this glasshouse.*

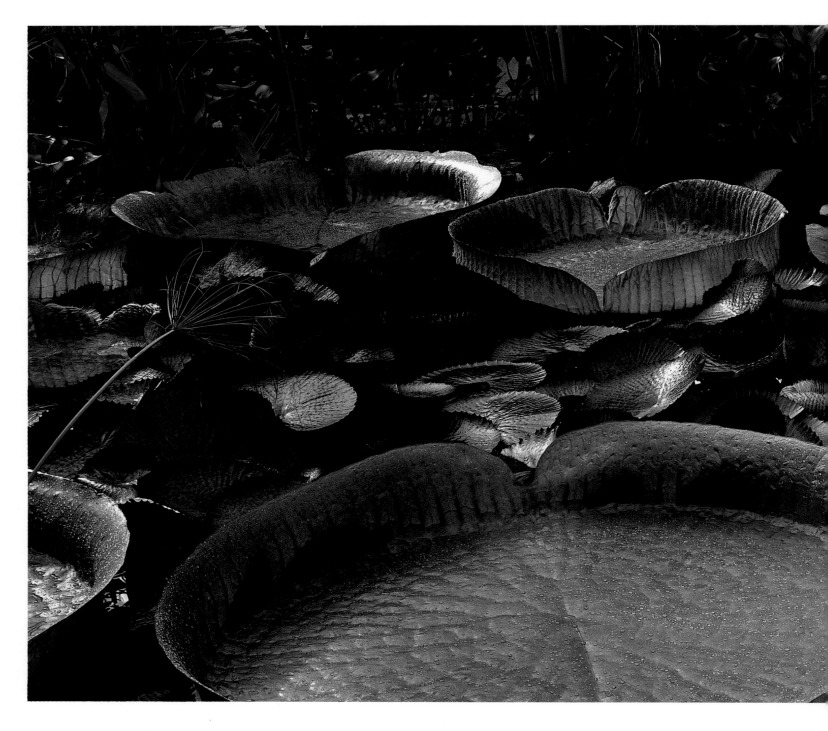

*Above: The giant leaves of* Victoria amazonica *are said to be capable of bearing the weight of a baby. They are about 1.2m (4 ft) across. The flowers are pale pink but only open for one night. Growing with* Victoria amazonica *is another smaller tropical water lily with rose-pink flowers.*

walls are crumbling, yet the forest of sub-tropical palms and giant creepers still reaches to the roof. The Orchid House, just to the right of the Palm House, is filled with an ever-expanding collection, but this too is under threat.

The Botanic Gardens run a three-year course teaching 150 students the academic and practical aspects of gardening. Sheltered by the Caucasian elm (*Zelkova carpinifolia*), there is an excellent library in a fine new building designed by Ciaran O'Connor. The National Herbarium (an archive for plants containing dried and documented specimens) contains over 600,000 examples of plants, including mosses, ferns, fungi and seaweeds, and provides essential reference sources for scholarly study as well as for the naming of plants and maintaining the standards of horticultural exactitude. The botanical library includes rare illustrated books, herbals dating from 1532, nursery catalogues, complete runs of botanical magazines, fascinating early botanic photographs, over 2,500 watercolour illustrations and records from notable Irish plant collectors, including Augustine Henry and Robert Lloyd Praeger.

To the left of the new library is the new Alpine House, sturdily built of Douglas fir in the proper old-fashioned shape. There are pans of brightly coloured alpines in tightly flowering mounds on gravel beds. Tiny climbers with tendrils clinging to a rock in a wet pan are labelled as coming from Dingle, Nepal, North America and Europe. Outside, alpines grow in beds within an enclosed garden with climbers on the walls. The overall impression is one of freshness and peace.

*Above: The sharp spiky fronds of a palm leaf set against the decaying joints holding together the panes of glass in the Great Palm House.*

*Opposite above: The Great Palm House built in 1884 is due to undergo a major restoration programme.*

*Opposite centre: Plume poppies (Macleaya microcarpa) and the Californian tree poppy (Romneya coulteri) in the Family Beds. These beds display plants related to one another. In the background is the Great Palm House.*

*Opposite below: The teak door of the Great Palm House – the wooden sashes are awaiting restoration.*

Moving on, you pass a group of cherries and a bed of every kind of japonica (*Chaenomeles*), until you arrive at a solid swathe of flowering bearded iris in spiky-leaved clumps of palest blue and violet darkening to purple flecked with yellow. Then a trellised circular walk held together by arches covered in different clematis encloses a group of magnolias. The plots of both the common and the exotic vegetables are enclosed by a tapestry hedge of different types of hollies. Another bed beyond is filled with pink-, white- and purple-flowered *Weigela* and then come the beds of deliciously scented mock orange, followed by the beds of species and garden varieties of *Deutzia* all planted together. A group of black locust (*Robinia pseudoacacia*) stands at the edge of the greenwood forest filled with oaks of every variety planted in shaded walks, separated from the Herb Garden by the Chinese Shrubbery.

Then there comes the glorious smell of pines and you find yourself at one end of two, long, old-fashioned Edwardian herbaceous borders, each one at least 3.5m (12ft) wide. A great swathe of colour sweeps up both sides of the path edged in boxwood, with flowers such as poppies, geraniums, lupins, the tiny blue *Veronica pinnata*, delphiniums and foxgloves. The sight is reminiscent of a painting by the Edwardian watercolourist Mildred Anne Butler. All this part of the garden is so sheltered by the pines, some of them among the earliest introductions here, that there is never a gust of wind.

Reginald Farrer, the nineteenth-century plant collector, described the Rock Garden in the Botanic Gardens as a 'Devil's Lapful'. He wrote, 'The plan is simplicity itself. You take a hundred or a thousand cartloads of bare, square-faced boulders. You next drop them all about absolutely anyhow; and you then plant things among them. The chaotic hideousness of the result is something to be remembered with shudders ever after.' This seems rather a severe indictment of this period piece undergoing renewal as I write. Walking through the dappled groves of trees, another period piece, the 'Chain Tent', catches your eye. Here you can sit under the 'tent', which is covered in wisteria, and look out, through the light filtered through the wisteria, onto the clear pond dotted with pink, yellow and white water lilies. Boxwood hedges hem in great clumps of wine-red peonies. A series of huge trees edge the water garden including the cucumber, hop and tulip trees – hellebores, Solomon's seal, Siberian iris, montbretia and day lilies all flourish far below their canopies. Across the River Tolka is a neatly laid out Rose Garden.

The Botanic Gardens at Glasnevin have always acted as the nerve centre of Irish gardening. They received seeds from the great plant-hunters' expeditions to the Far East, collating and recording them, growing them, and then distributing them to keen gardeners all over the country. The Moore family's connection with Glasnevin spanned nearly a century from 1838 to 1922, and during that time there wasn't a serious gardener on this island who didn't benefit in some way from their help and advice. The great Irish plant collector Augustine Henry has many of the plants he discovered in central China represented at Glasnevin, including *Emmenopterys henryi*. An earlier plant collector, James Tweedie, corresponded with Ninian Niven and David Moore, and sent to Glasnevin in the 1840s the first pampas grass, *Cortaderia selloana*, from Argentina. Edward Madden sent back the giant lily *Cardiocrinum giganteum* and also the scented *Abelia triflora*, an original seedling of which still thrives in front of the Fern House. Ernest 'Chinese' Wilson, who scoured China for the handkerchief tree, is remembered in the Chinese Shrubbery where plants still bear his collecting numbers. Some of the species rhododendrons that Charlotte Wheeler Cuffe painted in Burma in 1912 are doing well in the Curvilinear Range.

Among all the exotics that have been brought back at such cost of human endeavour from distant corners of the globe, there is perhaps one that no one would willingly pass by. Not loud or colourful, but just a small pink rose on a bush grown from a cutting taken from the one in an Irish garden at Jenkinstown near Kilkenny, *Rosa chinensis* 'Old Blush', Thomas Moore's inspiration for 'The Last Rose of Summer' (see page 159).

The Director, who has spent so much of his life working in the National Botanic Gardens, must have the last word. 'It is a complex place,' he explains. 'Gardens take a lifetime to make, and then they are hard to renew. In Victorian times, gardeners were skilled but not literate, but now our gardeners are fully qualified to take entire charge of collections. All the same, you can learn from the old gardeners. There was a period of resting, perhaps, when the general public weren't so interested, but gardening always went on in places like this – and now it has become a national pastime again.' In the 1830s, 20,000 visitors came each year when there were only a couple of dozen seats for them to sit on after they had walked the 5km (3 miles) from Dublin. Now visitor numbers are in excess of 100,000, and there are plenty of seats to sit on. Donal Synnott hopes that, with new facilities, such as a restaurant and lecture hall, and with the Curvilinear Range and Great Palm House restored, he can double the numbers of visitors each year to this splendid institution.

*Plan of National Botanic Gardens*

1. Mill Field
2. Rose Garden
3. Curvilinear Range
4. Succulent House
5. Aquatic Victoria House
6. Fern House
7. Alpine House
8. Orchid House
9. Great Palm House
10. Display House
11. Herbaceous Borders
12. Family Beds
13. Cherries
14. Annuals
15. Herb Garden
16. Chinese Shrubbery
17. Poisonous Plants
18. Rock Garden
19. Pond
20. River Tolka

# ROWALLANE

## COUNTY DOWN

The story of the gardens at Rowallane, County Down, famous today for their rhododendrons, starts with the sound of a sermon being preached on the back lawn. It is unlikely that the Revd John Moore could have foreseen the future of the Pleasure Grounds of his modest farmhouse when he acquired the property in 1858. His improvements to the estate, including the planting of pines and other conifers, provided the much-needed shelter and height for the garden that was to be made by his nephew Hugh Armytage Moore, who inherited the property in 1903. It is a relaxing garden to wander through, in part because the unpretentious layout of the original field pattern is still there, complete with ivy-covered walls and gates and soft springy turf. Informal paths lead through the different sections past stony outcrops of rock, down gentle declivities and up gradual slopes. The planting flows harmoniously across and around the lie of the land, gently covering the slopes and encroaching onto the rocks.

*Previous page, main picture: The stone pyramids of water-worn boulders – an unusual feature of the gardens at Rowallane were built by the Revd John Moore.*

*Previous page, detail: Wild maidenhair spleenworts cling to the stone walls.*

Lining the avenue on the approach to the house are giant cairns that the Revd John Moore built from piling up pyramids of huge round boulders, giving the first hint of the Victorian parson's craggy determination to leave his mark on the countryside that, when he arrived, was empty except for the furze and heather growing over the rocky fields. The avenue winds through the dark sumptuous plantings of conifers, beech and immense rhododendrons, so that you emerge into the light with the farmhouse, which is now the Regional Head Office of the National Trust in Northern Ireland, in front of you. Revd Moore built the stables and the Walled Gardens, in which he mainly grew vegetables and fruit. However, apart from the specimen conifers, the Pleasure Grounds and pond, he really concentrated on his oratory rather than on his gardening, leaving the creation of the garden that we see today to his nephew.

Not only did Hugh Armytage Moore have good taste in the plants that he chose, but he also knew instinctively where to place them, making good use of the lie and fall of the land. The fact that County Down has such an important

*Above left: A glimpse over a gate of the sea of rhododendrons that are Rowallane's glory in spring.*

*Above: Azaleas blossoming in the gardens at Rowallane.*

group of gardens is perhaps no coincidence since it was also the home of a number of outstanding nurseries, such as Slieve Donard and Daisy Hill, now alas defunct. These certainly contributed to the plant material of the gardens, as well as being of benefit to both garden owners and nurserymen who were able to exchange seeds, plants and knowledge. Also nearby, one of his sisters, Priscilla Cecilia, was planting what is now the National Arboretum. This fertile combination of circumstances, as well as the National Trust's continuing imaginative development, have all contributed to Rowallane's reputation as one of the most interesting gardens in the country.

Very little manmade landscaping has ever been carried out on the terrain, which coincides with William Robinson's theories of the importance of integrating garden plants into natural and semi-natural countryside. The soil is acid and thin, overlying whinstone rock, and, although at 100cm (40in) the rainfall is low for Ireland, the air is always humid, the winter frosts are not severe and the equable climate provides ideal growing conditions. Hugh

Armytage Moore was fortunate to inherit Rowallane at the beginning of one of the most exciting periods for gardening in Ireland and Britain. New plants were flooding in, especially from the Far East, collected by the intrepid plant-hunters, such as Ernest Wilson and Frank Kingdon Ward. He corresponded with them and subscribed to their expeditions, so he was able to raise many rare plants from their seeds, and these seedlings were planted all over the garden. With such a wealth of new material, 'accidents' were bound to happen, and some of the accidental seedlings, hybrids of unrecorded parentage, turned out to be superb garden plants. To Rowallane's bees we owe the scarlet-blossomed quince *Chaenomeles* x *superba* 'Rowallane Seedling', and the striking yellow St John's-wort *Hypericum* 'Rowallane Hybrid'. The candelabra primrose *Primula* 'Rowallane Rose', was also a chance seedling. On the other hand, the Rowallane viburnum, *Viburnum plicatum* f. *tomentosum* 'Rowallane Seedling', was probably just one of the countless seedlings raised from the collectors' lots. Moore planted an abundance of azaleas and the larger rhododendrons, including the fragrant, late-flowering white *Rhododendron auriculatum* from central China, drifts of naturalized bulbs, and many unusual trees. In 1942 the Royal Horticultural Society awarded him the Victoria Medal of Honour for his work in his garden.

Starting at The Haggard where in midsummer the cottony seeds of the Japanese poplar (*Populus maximowiczii*), cover the ground like snow, you walk through the gate to the Spring Ground. Here, in early Spring, old Irish cultivars of thin-petalled, daffodils cover the grassy knolls. These are followed by the wild flowers among the grass, such as primroses, violet, butterfly

*Opposite: A gate pier of jagged stone work beneath the tracery of branches that form the overhanging canopy of forest trees.*

*Opposite below: One of the small gates that still remain in the network of walls that divided the different fields in the original layout of the Revd John Moore's pasture lands.*

*Below:* Primula *'Rowallane Rose' was a chance seedling at Rowallane. It is proudly planted in a rockery, below a boulder that sports a flowery clump of London pride.*

orchids, spotted orchids and horned poppy, and later by colonies of blue devil's-bit scabious, as well as the unusual American blue-eyed grass (*Sisyrinchium angustifolium*). Visitors flock to this area of the garden, perhaps because it is a reminder of the days when drifts of colour spread across hedge, ditch and field in spring all over the country.

At the end of the glade, there is a spring time explosion of colour from the massed banks of azaleas and rhododendrons, which are sheltered by pine, beech and oak. Specimen trees, such as Dawyck beech, stewartias and a bright-red-fruited crab apple (*Malus sargentii*) lead you to the famous Rock Garden, where Hugh Armytage Moore dug out and displayed an outcrop of stone, polished and scraped by glaciers thousands of years ago. Rhododendrons are everywhere and the beautiful *Primula* 'Rowallane Rose' flourishes in groups of perennials by the streams.

In the Hospital there is a group of trees that are all native to the forests of the Andes, but which are equally at home at Rowallane. The great southern beech (*Nothofagus dombeyii*) towers above the huge bush of *Desfontainea spinosa*, with its prickly holly-like leaves and yellow-mouthed scarlet tubular flowers. A handsome *Cladrastris lutea*, the Kentucky yellow-wood, with wisteria-like panicles of scented white blossom stands next to the lady of the woods (*Betula pendula*) and *Lomatia ferruginea*. A huge handkerchief tree (*Davidia involucrata*) spreads its branches laden with the white bracts that give it its English name, and ferns and foxgloves thrive beneath the canopy.

The L-shaped Outer Walled Garden is one of the most sheltered places in the garden, with the sun beaming into it over the range of beech and lime trees that shield it from the wind. The walls are made of bands of brick and stone with porcelain tiles projecting out, enabling wires to be threaded through to tie up the plants. *Philadelphus* 'Burfordensis' leans over a seat with the scent of *P.* 'Belle Etoile' drifting from around the corner. The South American pineapple guava (*Feijoa sellowiana*), with crimson-and-white flowers, fills one corner and a euchrypia stands amid hydrangeas.

Holding aside a curtain of wisteria to walk through a gate, you come to the Inner Walled Garden, where the National Collection of Penstemon is enclosed by hedges of boxwood clipped into cubes at each corner. In the centre of the next part of the garden, which is designed in the shape of a Celtic cross, stands the original plant of Rowallane's own viburnum. A gate lies ahead, leading onto crisply edged mown lawns, which beckon you towards the Pleasure Grounds at the back of the house.

During the Second World War, the number of gardeners diminished and many of the best-loved features became overgrown. The fact that the garden survived this period is due to the care and attention of the National Trust, which acquired the property in 1954 and orchestrated a strong and imaginative development programme. It was also due to the work of Lady O'Neill of the Maine who was instrumental in rescuing it, and after her to Graham Stuart Thomas, and then John Sales, as well as to the head gardeners of the past and to Mike Snowden, the Head Gardener of today.

*Plan of Rowallane Gardens*

① The Haggard
② Spring Ground
③ Rock Garden
④ Hospital
⑤ Outer Walled Garden
⑥ Inner Walled Garden
⑦ Pleasure Grounds
⑧ Pond

# WOODFIELD
## COUNTY OFFALY

Dr Keith Lamb's private garden which surrounds his eighteenth-century house at Woodfield, Clara, County Offaly, is a secret, magical place of many parts, vibrant with plantlife. The house and garden, deep in the countryside near the Bog of Clara, have a settled, remote quality. An enchanting map of the demesne of Woodfield is illustrated with a watercolour showing the pedimented house as it was in 1765, with an embroidered formal garden enclosed in hedges with topiary, a hop yard, an orchard and plantations of trees set in fields. The great bog is clearly marked. A fair-haired huntsman with his hounds chases a graceful fox across the top of the illustration, while a stag dashes off to the right, and the whole map is bordered by a ribbon of flowers including fritillaries, tulips and roses, ancestors perhaps of some of the many flowers that flourish at Woodfield today.

*Previous page, main picture: In many Irish gardens, texture is as important as colour. The grey rough limestone walls of the old farm buildings provide the perfect back drop for the simple plain green fronds of a bank of ferns.*

*Previous page, detail: Blue-eyed Mary, (Omphalodes cappadocica) is just one of the many beautiful plants that thrives at Woodfield.*

Twenty-five years ago, Dr Keith Lamb joined the Kinsealy Horticultural Research Station as Chief Horticultural Research Officer. After a short time spent working on glasshouse crops, he started the Horticultural Nursery Stock Department, which dealt with the propagation and culture of trees and shrubs. Among his many achievements were his successful experiments proving that camellias would grow on moderately limy soil. With two other colleagues, he wrote the *Nursery Stock Manual*, the basic handbook used by all nurserymen, adding to his reputation in the horticultural world. He wrote his thesis on the neglected subject of Irish apples, which involved endless travelling around the counties of Ireland documenting the varieties of apples that he found in old orchards. He is a past president of the Royal Horticultural Society of Ireland and received their Medal of Honour in 1982 (which was a unique medal designed by Wendy Walsh and decorated with a fritillary). More recently, with Patrick Bowe, he has written *A History of Gardening in Ireland*, the only book available about the development of gardening in Ireland from prehistoric times to the present day. Despite all these accolades, Dr Lamb possesses a modest diffidence of character, which is reflected in the intimacy of his garden at Woodfield. All the different elements around the house have been kept as they were, and he and his wife Helen have interleaved the garden very gently using the old trees as shelter.

When his older brother Adam died a bachelor, Dr Lamb decided to retire early in order to live at Woodfield. He was delighted to find a totally overgrown Rockery, an ideal place to grow alpines – one of his great interests. The Lambs have travelled with the Alpine Garden Society to different mountain ranges to study the living conditions of the plants. In what had been the Kennel Yard behind the house, he built a series of eight raised beds, providing the well-drained soil that alpines enjoy in their native habitats. One of the unique features of Irish alpine gardening is the number of plants from the southern hemisphere that flourish here and Dr Lamb has had great success growing plants from Patagonia, New Zealand and South Africa, alongside Irish natives and North American and Himalayan species.

In an area of under an acre, he has recreated in miniature all the sections you would expect to find in a much larger Irish garden. The old woodland avenue has been made into a garden. A wild garden has been developed inside the grey stone walls of the Old Bawn. Many plants were given by and exchanged with a spreading network of gardening friends, from Lord Talbot de Malahide of Malahide Castle, and Lady Moore at Rathfarnham in the old days, to Helen Dillon and Jim Reynolds today. The cheerful ghosts of old friends and their stories are attached to many of the plants that live on at Woodfield in their memory.

In early spring, the bare trunks and tangled branches of the ancient beech trees are underplanted with a brilliant carpet of bulbs. There are lots of different snowdrops, from the common wild snowdrop (*Galanthus nivalis*), both single and double, to the extraordinary 'Scharlockii', which looks as if it has acquired a pair of donkey's ears. Dr Lamb also grows the lovely Irish

snowdrop 'Straffan', which arose at Straffan House in County Kildare when
a snowdrop said to have been brought back from the Crimea by Major Eyre
Massey after the Crimean War was crossed with the common one. The many
daffodils include two dwarf ones, *Narcissus nanus* and *N. cyclamineus*, both
from northern Spain and Portugal, which Dr Lamb himself cross-pollinated
to produce 'Fairy Gold', a very pretty, prolific and free-blooming golden-
flowered miniature with a frilled trumpet. 'Fairy Gold' was only named and
officially registered in 1998, although he had produced it in the early 1940s.
Then there are the blue, white, double white and yellow wood anemones,
followed by spring-flowering cyclamen. Here are the speckled grey-green
patterned leaves of *Cyclamen repandum,* with carmine flowers spotted and
rimmed with red. Beneath the spreading branches of an old yew tree, the
pink blossoms of *C. libanoticum* are quite at home even though far from
their Lebanese home. Indeed, cyclamen from all around the Mediterranean
nestle beneath the trees of Woodfield. *C. balearicum* from Majorca and
nearby islands produces fragrant flowers each spring, while a Turkish species,
*C. cilicium*, has slender pink and white blossoms in autumn. Also in that
season, the familiar *C. hederifolium* carpets the woodland garden, its delicate
pink petals folded back like slim butterfly wings.

In spring and early summer, the woodland garden is awash with trinity
flowers. The grandest one is the pure white *Trillium grandiflorum*, whose
flowers often flush pink before the petals fall, and the most precious one
is the rare double-flowered form of it. The Californian wake robin (*Trillium*

*Opposite: Trilliums and dog tooth violets
(Erythronium) grow with great vigour at
Woodfield, in the glades beneath the canopy
of beech trees.*

*Above: Early spring – trout lilies, daffodils and
hellebores are in bloom while the beech trees still
have not sprouted new leaves.*

*Above: It is hard to believe that this was once a kennel yard. Keith Lamb built the eight raised beds and now it is an alpine wonderland with hundreds of different plants; some clinging, some creeping, some tumbling near the edge and all in superb condition.*

*chloropetalum*), has red-and-white, pale pink and dark red flowers and is so content at Woodfield that it has seeded itself and is spreading over the limestone gravel of the drive. Dr Lamb does not confine his trilliums to the woodland garden though. In several of the stone troughs that are so typical of Irish country gardens, he grows the dwarf snow wake robin (*Trillium nivale*), which is just 13cm (5in) tall and, though generally difficult to please, here has also seeded itself.

At the top of the drive, near the house, is the original tree of a beautiful white-blossomed cherry which flowers very early in the year. This is 'Woodfield Cluster', which Dr Lamb raised himself in the 1940s. He had gathered fruit from a cherry tree growing in the grounds of the Albert College at Glasnevin, not far from the National Botanic Gardens, and this was one of the resulting seedlings. The weeping branches are thickly covered with deep rose-pink buds by the beginning of spring and when they open the petals are pure white.

Turning left into the old walled garden you pass a pink rambling rose and to get into The Bawn – a verdant jungle. A mock orange (*Philadephus*) scents the air, and the ground is thick with primroses and foxgloves. This is a place where leaves count as much as flowers. The Chilean rhubarb throws gigantic green umbrellas over acanthus and pink-plumed rodgersias. The ivory trumpets of the Himalayan lily (*Cardiocrinum giganteum*) light up the green steamy shade; each spire is taller than the average gardener and bears about a dozen scented flowers. The spiky purple-leaved cabbage palm (*Cordyline australis*) presents a stark contrast, while the brilliant blue flowers of a *Corydalis flexuosa* catch the eye nearby. An *Arisaema* from the Himalayas, still only labelled with a collector's number, flourishes next to the white form of *Meconopsis*, whose flowers sway elegantly on slender stems. The climbing white rose that hangs over the empty stone window of the roofless stable came as a cutting from the last owner of Rosefield where the Blackrock Clinic in Dublin now stands. In early spring, fresh green beech leaves provide the interest within the window frame, followed by the equally arresting tumbling summer roses and autumn sunsets. Ferns flourish both inside the stable and around the outside walls.

When I visited the Lambs, a great 3.5m (12ft) high bugloss (*Echium pininana*) was flourishing by the front door of Woodfield, its bright blue flower spike lending an exotic touch to the simple lawn and the meadows beyond. But the bugloss, from the Canary Islands, dies after it has flowered so it is unlikely to be seen again; it does however seed itself. Nearby, a *Cornus kousa*, whose white petals are tinged with pink, arrived as a seedling. Honeysuckle and wisteria climb the walls of the house, sheltered by beech trees and surrounded by a small border. In the old fernery, there are hardy ferns of all sorts, including maidenhairs and hart's-tongues and one that looks like a very healthy clump of the curliest parsley. The fernery melds into the rockery, where every piece of ground is covered with contented plants, their pink, purple, white, violet, blue and green starry faces glowing among the rocks. A stunning gentian – it has never been properly named – with flowers

*Below: Not a single inch of space has been wasted in this garden – climbers cover the walls and even the nooks and crannies have been planted with succulent houseleeks.*

the colour of lapis lazuli forms a perfect wreath. Dr Lamb obtained this gentian many years ago from the National Botanic Gardens at Glasnevin and, since it never sets seed, he has propagated it each year by taking cuttings. The sweetly scented pink-and-white-striped spathe of *Arisaema candidissimum* is near *A. costatum* from China, looking as if it was made from stripy chocolate. The deep blue saucers of the mat-forming prostrate speedwell *Veronica prostrata* 'Trehane' carpet the rocks in front of the intensely yellow flower heads of the South African thistle *Berkheya macrocephela*.

In a sheltered nook against the house there are many other treasured plants, including colonies of the sumptuous blue poppy *Meconopsis* x *sheldonii*, hardy orchids such as the purple-flowered Kilmarnock orchid, which has densely spotted leaves, and the Russian foxglove. In a trough is a campanula, originally from Tully Nursery near Kildare when it belonged to Lord Wavertree. The head gardener was W.H.Paine, and so the purple flowers splashed with white were called after him. The airy perennial *Aquilegia formosa* with orange spires and yellow petals lines the peppermint-covered path, and a dark pink rose is tangled in syringa. A little sundial is ringed by a solid band of flowering geranium. An old yew shades the path edged by hellebores and ferns and a strange plant whose leaves when bruised seem to smell of fox. The white baneberry (*Actaea alba*) flourishes in this shade and the black-and-white berries do indeed look like dolls' eyes, its other name.

All along the sunny south-facing wall of the old kennel yard hang different clematis, such as 'Rouge Cardinal' with single crimson flowers and 'Lasurstern' with large blue ones. Hundreds of different plants are gathered here in the raised beds, including the insect-catching American pitcher plant

*Below: In spring under the beech trees there is a multicoloured carpet of Magenta cyclamen, blue-and-white wood anemones and clumps of daffodils.*

(*Sarracenia purpurea*) and its Californian cousin, the cobra lily (*Darlingtonia californica*). Although it is not a native Irish plant, the extraordinary pitcher plant is now found growing on a number of Irish bogs, including nearby Woodfield Bog, having been deliberately planted out over fifty years ago. At Woodfield the cobra lilies and pitcher plants share a peat-filled raised bed – a miniature bog – with heathers from Spain, cranberries and the beautiful pink-flowered bog rosemary (*Andromeda polifolia*).

Dr Charles Nelson, the taxonomist at the Botanic Gardens at Glasnevin for several decades, has written prolifically about many areas of gardening. In his book *An Irish Flower Garden Replanted* he drew attention to one of the most remarkable Irish ferns surviving from the Victorian era. It was found by a Mrs Frizell in the mid-nineteenth century growing between two large boulders on the Avonmore River at Castle Kevin in County Wicklow. It is known as the tatting fern because its fronds resemble the edging of pieces of lace, conjuring up a picture of a determined and conscientious Victorian lady with hat, trowel and trug. In the shadiest part of the old kennel yard at Woodfield, there is a bed specially for miniature ferns, including Mrs Frizell's elegant monstrosity.

The raised beds are in their prime in late spring and early summer. Little fritillaries and New Zealand mountain daisies (*Celmisia*) in variety mingle with dwarf irises, gentians and phloxes. Over the side of one there is a cascading carpet of mountain avens (*Dryas octopetala*). This form is another Woodfield speciality and has recently been named 'Burren Nymph' because Dr Lamb found it in the Burren where mountain avens grow in profusion. The flowers are double with many more than the expected eight petals, so they look like small white roses. 'Burren Nymph' came to Woodfield as a cutting and has proved its worth, so it is being multiplied by a local nursery for sale to gardeners everywhere. In another bed, southern hemisphere forget-me-nots with white and yellow, not blue, flowers flourish. Even the walls themselves are used – succulent houseleeks (*Sempervivum*) and fairy foxgloves (*Erinus alpinus*) grow in the cracks.

Standing at the back courtyard of the house with three lacy trees of *Robinia* x *hillieri* planted in the yard with their wisteria-like panicles, with stone troughs full of plants, a white-walled slate-roofed barn, lilies in pots, lots more pots, a little greenhouse and a glimpse of the rose through the empty stone window, one is struck by the feeling of activity and at the same time stability. It is obvious that this garden belongs to a man who has both peace of mind and clarity of thought. Although deaf from his youth, he misses nothing and can lipread perfectly. He assures me that every single plant is in the best available position, and that each one gives its owner a lot of pleasure. As I am leaving Woodfield, Dr Lamb gestures to a low, evergreen shrub bearing pink flowers positively bursting out of its trough. '*Philesia magellanica*,' he explains gently, and then with a wry smile and a twinkle in his eye, 'usually regarded as rather difficult to grow ...' which is probably as near to a boast as he'll ever get.

*Above: Shuttlecock ferns are so called because of their resemblance to the feathered shuttlecock used in the game of badminton. They are emerging from their winter covering in the roofless barn.*

# VISITOR'S GUIDE

## ALTAMONT

Tullow, Co. Carlow

T 353 50 35 9444

F 353 50 35 9128

**Opening Times:** April–October

Please check before visiting.

**Facilities:** toilets; teas; craft shop; garden centre
with unusual plants; potager & herb garden;
art gallery; wheelchair access.

## ANNES GROVE

Castletownroche, Co. Cork

T 353 22 26145

F 353 22 26145

**Opening Times:** Mid-March–September

**Facilities:** toilets; buffet meals; guided tours
by appointment; wheelchair access.

## ARDCARRAIG

Bushy Park, Oranswell, Co. Galway

T 353 91 524336

**Opening Times:** Open strictly by appointment.

Not suitable for wheelchairs or dogs;

**Facilities:** toilets.

## BALLINLOUGH CASTLE GARDENS

Clonmellon, Co. Westmeath

T 353 46 33135

F 353 46 33331

**Opening Times:** May–September. Other times
by arrangement. Closed first two weeks in August.

**Facilities:** toilets; plants for sale; teas; guided tours
by arrangement; limited wheelchair access.

## BALLYMALOE COOKERY SCHOOL GARDENS

Shanagarry, Middleton, Co. Cork

T 353 21 646785

F 353 21 646909

**Opening Times:** April–September

**Facilities:** toilets; guided tours; garden café
and shop; limited wheelchair access.

## BIRR CASTLE

Rosse Row, Birr, Co. Offaly

T 353 50 92 0336

F 353 50 92 1583

**Opening Times:** All year round

**Facilities:** toilets; guided tours; coffee shop;
gift shop; plants for sale; wheelchair access.

## BUTTERSTREAM

Trim, Co. Meath

T 353 46 36017

F 353 46 31702

**Opening Times:** April–September daily.

**Facilities:** toilets; plants for sale; teas;
wheelchair access.

## CREAGH

Skibbereen, Co. Cork

T 353 28 22121

F 353 28 22121

**Opening Times:** March–October daily.

Closed Tuesdays. Other times by appointment.

**Facilities:** toilets; teas; wheelchair access;
guided tours by arrangement.

## DERREEN

Lauragh, Killarney, Co.Kerry

T 353 64 83588

**Opening Times:** April– October.

Other times by appointment.

**Facilities:** toilets; teas; picnic area;
guided tours for groups.

*Left to right: Altamont, Birr Castle,*
*Butterstream, Glin Castle, Kilfane Glen*
*and Waterfall, Mount Stewart.*

## THE DILLON GARDEN

45, Sandford Road, Ranelagh, Dublin 6

T 353 1 4971308

F 353 1 4971308

**Opening Times**: March, July and August daily; April, June and September Sundays only

**Facilities**: toilets; plants for sale; guided tours by appointment.

## GLENVEAGH CASTLE

Glenveagh National Park, Co. Donegal

T 353 74 37088

F 353 74 37072

**Opening Times**: April–October

**Facilities**: toilets; teas.

## GLIN CASTLE

Pleasure Ground & Walled Garden, Co. Limerick

T 353 68 34173

F 353 68 34364

**Opening Times**: Gardens by appointment only.

**Facilities**: toilets; parking; shop in gate lodge; limited wheelchair access; luxury accommodation available in castle.

## ILNACULLIN

Glengariff, Co. Cork

T 353 27 63040

**Opening Times**: March–October

**Facilities**: toilets; teas.

## KILFANE GLEN & WATERFALL

Thomastown, Co. Kilkenny

T 353 56 24588

F 353 56 27491

**Opening Times**: May–September. Other times by appointment.

**Facilities**: toilets; teas; car park; guided tours by arrangement.

## KILLRUDDERY

Bray, Co. Wicklow

T 353 1 2862777

F 353 1 2862777

**Opening Times**: Gardens: April–September House: May, June and September. Groups and other dates and times by arrangement.

**Facilities**: toilets; wheelchair access.

## MOUNT STEWART

Newtownards, Co. Down

T 012477 88387

F 012477 88569

**Opening Times**: Formal garden March–September Lakeside gardens and walks May–September

**Facilities**: toilets; teas; wheelchair access.

## MOUNT USHER

Ashford, Co. Wicklow

T 353 404 40116/40205

F 353 404 40205

**Opening Times**: March–October

**Facilities**: toilets; teas; shops; parking; wheelchair access; guided tours can be booked in advance.

## NATIONAL BOTANIC GARDENS

Glasnevin, Dublin 9

T 353 1 8374388

F 353 1 83 60080

**Opening Times**: Daily all year.

**Facilities**: toilets; parking (limited); wheelchair access.

## ROWALLANE

Saintfield, Co. Down, BT24 7LH

T 028 9751 0131

**Opening Times**: April–October

**Facilities**: toilets; teas; wheelchair access.

## WOODFIELD

Clara, Co. Offaly

T 353 50 631161

**Opening Times**: Open to garden clubs strictly by appointment. Not open to general public.

**Facilities**: Cars can park at the rear of the house but coaches stay at the road – 400m away.

# INDEX

Page numbers in *italics* indicate illustrations.

# BIBLIOGRAPHY

Aalen, F.H.A., Whelan Kevin, Stout Matthew editors, *Atlas of the Irish Rural Landscape*, Cork 1997.

Annesley, Earl, *Beautiful and Rare Trees and Plants*, Privately printed 1903.

Barnard, T.C. 'Gardening, Diet and 'Improvement' in Later Seventeenth Century Ireland' *Journal of Garden History* 10, (1) 71–75. (1990).

Bean, W.J. *Trees and Shrubs Hardy in the British Isles*, London 1970–6.

Bisgrove, Richard, *The Gardens of Gertrude Jekyll*, London 1992.

Bence-Jones, Mark, *A Guide to Irish Country Houses*, Revised edition, London 1988.

Bowe, P.T.P. and Nelson E.C. (editors), 'A list of gardens and parks of international and national significance in the Republic of Ireland' (January 1988), *Moorea* 7: 5–15 (1988)

Butler, Hubert, *Escape from the Anthill*, Mullingar 1981.

Butler, Hubert, *In the Land of Nod*, Dublin 1996.

Casey, C. and Rowan, A., *North Leinster, the counties of Longford, Louth, Meath and Westmeath*, London 1993.

Connolly, Sybil and Dillon, Helen, editors, *In An Irish Garden*, London 1986.

Cornforth, John, 'Ballinlough Castle', *Country Life* 13th.July, (1978).

Cornforth, John, & Glin, 'Knight of, Killruddery,' *Country Life*, (1977).

Day, Angelique, editor, *Letters from Georgian Ireland, The Correspondence of Mary Delany 1731–68*.

Dillon, Helen, *The Flower Garden*, London 1993.

Dillon, Helen, *Garden Artistry*, New York 1995.

Dillon, Helen, *On Gardening*, Dublin 1998.

Fabricant, Carol, *Swifts' Landscape*, Baltimore 1982.

Fallon, Brian, *An Age of Innocence*, Dublin, 1998.

Fingal, Countess of, *Seventy Years Young*, London 1937.

FitzMaurice Mills, J. *The Noble Dwellings of Ireland*, London 1987.

Forest, Mary, *Trees and shrubs cultivated in Ireland* Kilkenny: Heritage Gardens Committee, An Taisce 1985.

Foster, R.F., editor, *The Oxford Illustrated History of Ireland*, Oxford 1989.

Foster, John Wilson, editor, *Nature in Ireland*, Dublin 1997.

Froude, J.A. *Short Studies on Great Subjects*, London 1871.

George, Michael, and Bowe, Patrick, *The Gardens of Ireland*, London 1986.

Glin, Knight of, and Bowe, P.T.P. (editors) *Gardens of outstanding historic interest in the Republic of Ireland*, The Republic of Ireland ICOMOS Committee 1980.

Guinness, Desmond and Ryan, William, *Irish Houses & Castles*, London 1971.

Heggarty, Maureen, 'Kilfane' *Old Kilkenny Review* 7–20 1974.

Heron, Marianne, *The Hidden Gardens of Ireland*, Revised edition, Dublin 1996.

Howley, J. *The Follies and Garden Buildings of Ireland*, London 1993.

Hussey, Christopher, *The Life of Sir Edwin Lutyens*, Vols 1–3 London 1950.

Hyams, Edward, *Irish Gardens*, London 1967.

Jackson-Stops, Gervase, *An English Arcadia 1600–1990*, London 1992.

Jekyll, G. *Colour Planning of the Garden*, London 1924.

Jekyll, G. *Wall and Water Gardens*, London 1901.

Jekyll, G. *Wood and Garden*, London 1899.

Jupp, Belinda, *Heritage gardens inventory* 1992, Northern Ireland Heritage Gardens Committee.

Lacey, Stephen, *Gardens of the National Trust*, London 1996.

Lansdowne, Marquis of, *Glanerought and the Petty FitzMaurices*, Oxford 1937.

Lamb, J.G.D., and Bowe, P.T.P., *A History of Gardening in Ireland*, Dublin 1995.

Llanover, Lady, editor, *Autobiography and Correspondence of Mary Granville, Mrs.Delany*, London 1861 6 vols.

Londonderry, Marchioness of, *Retrospect*, London 1938.

Lord, James, *A Gift for Admiration*, New York 1998.

McCracken, Eileen, *The Irish Woods since Tudor Times*, Devon 1971.

Malins, E. and the Knight of Glin, *Lost Demesnes*, London 1976.

Malins E. and Bowe P. *Irish Gardens and their Demesnes from 1830*, London 1980.

Martin, Peter, *Pursuing Innocent Pleasures. The Gardening World of Alexander Pope*, Connecticut 1984.

Neeson, Eoin, *A History of Irish Forestry*, Dublin 1991.

Nelson, Charles, and Brady, Aiden, *Irish Gardening and Horticulture*, Dublin 1979.

Nelson, E.Charles, and Walsh, Wendy, *An Irish Flower Garden Replanted*, Castlebourke 1997.

Nelson, E.Charles & McCracken E.M., *The brightest jewel, a history of the National Botanic Gardens, Glasnevin Dublin*, Kilkenny 1987.

Nelson, E.Charles, *Shamrock*, Kilkenny 1991.

Nelson, E.C. & Grills, A., *Daisy Hill Nursery, Newry*, Belfast 1998.

Niven, Ninian, *The Visitors Companion to the Botanic Gardens in Glasnevin* Dublin 1838.

*Northern gardens and parks of outstanding historic interest in Northern Ireland*, Belfast: Ulster Architectural Heritage Society 1982.

O'Toole, Jimmy, *The Carlow Gentry*, Carlow 1993.

Ottewill, David, *The Edwardian Garden*, New Haven and London 1989.

Pakenham, Thomas, *Meetings with Remarkable Trees*, London 1996.

Pim, Sheila, *The Wood and the Trees, A Biography of Augustine Henry*, London 1996.

Reeves-Smyth, Terence, *Irish Gardens and Gardening Before Cromwell*, Kinsale 1999.

Reeves-Smyth, Terence, *Irish Gardens* Appletree Guide 1994 Belfast.

Reeves-Smyth, Terence, *A Historic Parks and Gardens Record for Ireland*, Carrickfergus 1991.

Robinson, William, *The English Flower Garden*, November 1883.

Robinson, William, *The Wild Garden*, London 1870.

Somerville Large, Peter, *The Coast of West Cork*, Belfast 1991.

Taylor, Patrick, *Daily Telegraph Gardens Guide to Britain and Ireland*, London 1998.

Thomas, Graham Stuart, *Gardens of the National Trust*, London 1979.

Thomas, Graham Stuart, *Cuttings From My Garden Notebooks*, New York 1997.

Walpole,E.H.editor *Recollections of Mount Usher 1868–1952*, Dublin 1952.

Walsh, Ursula Louise *Garden Restoration in Ireland: A Case Study, Ballinlough Castle*, Dublin 1995.

Walsh, W.F. & Nelson, E.C., *An Irish florilegium; the wild and gardens flowers of Ireland*, London 1983.

Walsh, W. F. & Nelson, E.C. *An Irish florilegium 11; the wild and gardens flowers of Ireland*, London 1988.

Watkin, David *The Life and Works of C.R.Cockerell*. London 1974.

White, Roger editor *Georgian Arcadia*, London 1987.

Williamson, Tom *Polite Landscapes*, Stroud 1995.

Wilson, C. Anne *The Country House Kitchen Garden 1600–1950*, London 1998.

Yeats, William Butler *Collected Poems*, London 1933.

**Publisher's Acknowledgments**

The publisher would like to thank Maggie Gowan and The National Trust Photographic Library.

The Slide File for the photographs that appear on pages 12, 13, 16, 20, 21.

First published in 1999
by Conran Octopus Limited
a part of Octopus Publishing Group
2–4 Heron Quays, London E14 4JP
www.conran-octopus.co.uk

This paperback edition published in 2002

Text copyright © Olda FitzGerald 1999
Design and layout copyright © Conran Octopus 1999
Photography © Stephen Robson 1999
Garden Plans © William Pounds 1999
Map of Ireland © Lesley Craig 1999

**Commissioning Editor**  Stuart Cooper
**Editor**  Helen Woodhall
**Editorial Assistant**  Alexandra Kent
**Copy Editor**  Annie Reid
**Index**  Helen Snaith

**Art Editor**  Isabel de Cordova/Pep Sala
**Picture Research**  Jessica Walton
**Illustrator**  William Pounds
**Production**  Oliver Jeffreys

British Library Cataloguing-in-Publication Data
A catalogue record for this book is available from the British Library

Colour origination by Sang Choy International, Singapore. Printed in China.

ISBN 1 84091 288 X